TURN BACK

YOUR BODY CLOCK

The Guide to Changing Your Life and Living

D0730894

With an Introduction by Dr Una Coales

by Carina Norris

From Celador Productions as seen on Channel Four

headline

First published in 2006
By HEADLINE BOOK PUBLISHING

10 9 8 7 6 5 4 3 2 1

Cataloguing in Publication Data is available from the British Library

ISBN 0 7553 1548 0

Typset in Univers and Impact
Photography by Paul Bricknell
Design by Fiona Pike
Pictures pp. 7, 147, 157 and 187 Getty Images
Printed and bound in Great Britain by CPI Bath

HEADLINE BOOK PUBLISHING
A division of HodderHeadline
338 Euston Road
London NW1 3BH

www.headline.co.uk
www.hodderheadline.com

Every effort has been made to ensure that the information in this book is accurate. The information in this book will be relevant to the majority of people but may not be applicable in each individual case so it is advised that professional medical advice is obtained for specific information on personal health matters. Neither the publisher nor Celador accept any legal responsibility for any personal injury or other loss or damage arising from the use or misuse of the information and advice in this book. Anyone making a change in their diet should consult their GP, especially if pregnant, infirm, elderly or under 16.

The publisher would like to thank Hertfordshire Sports Village, University of Hertfordshire. And a special thanks to the Turn Back Your Body Clock production team, especially Yvette Dore, Kirsty Hanson and Damon Pattison.

contents

meet the experts

Dr Una Coales BA (Hons), MD, FRCS, FRCS (ORL), DRCOG, DFFP, MRCGP

Dr Una Coales is a New York City surgeon turned medical writer for the Royal Society of Medicine, medical doctor and GP. She trained at The Johns Hopkins University in Baltimore, Maryland, USA and practised general surgery at St Luke's-Roosevelt Hospital (affiliated with Columbia University School of Medicine), a level-one trauma centre in New York City.

After relocating to London she attained the Fellowship of the Royal College of Surgeons in 1999 in general surgery and a second Fellowship in ear, nose and throat surgery in 2000. She worked as a surgeon for the NHS until 2001 when she retrained as a GP. She then gained the DFFP (diploma from the Faculty of Family Planning), the DRCOG (diploma from the Royal College of Obstetrics and Gynaecology) and the MRCGP (member of the Royal College of General Practitioners). She now works in South London as a GP and GP educator, teaching GPs to pass their UK licensing exam (MRCGP), and is a member of the board of the South London Faculty of the RCGP.

Una is a regular commentator on medical issues and was the medical expert and advisor on Channel 4's The Fit Farm (2004). She has also contributed to BBC Radio 4's You and Yours.

Tim Bean FLN, NSCA

Tim, an award-winning health club owner of 15 years, has implemented cutting-edge body transformation programmes. As co-owner of the Institute of Physique Management he has an impressive list of celebrity and international clients.

Carina Norris MSc (Dist), ANutr

Nutrition consultant, author and journalist Carina Norris studied biology followed by Public Health Nutrition. She has a passion to spread the word on healthy twenty-first century living and to help people de-junk their diets – the fun way.

introduction

by Dr Una Coales

Did you know that someone in the UK has a heart attack every two minutes? That the incidence of deaths from bowel cancer in the UK is the equivalent of a jumbo jet crash every week? And that tobacco kills more than 300 people each day?

As you approach forty, it's pretty common to sense the clock is ticking and that you're running out of time. You may well ask yourself, how long have I got left? And I'm afraid the answer may well be, not as long as you think.

This book, published alongside the Channel 4 series Turn Back Your Body Clock, will work with you to assess your diet and lifestyle and, within sound medical parameters, help you work out how long you've got left. It's a practical guide to combating the ageing process and improving on your death age.

You may not like what you hear. You may be in denial. But it's my job both as a GP and a surgeon to bring your relationship with your mortality up close and personal. If you can commit to making some achievable changes to your life, then the news is good. Premature death can be avoided. You can live longer, and you can live better.

Now, I know what you're thinking. You're thinking, 'I am still young. It could never happen to me. I am only in my thirties…' Well, think again. All you need to live longer – and to live more healthily – is someone to tell you how. And that's where the Turn Back Your Body Clock team comes in.

I have met people who could have lived longer and enjoyed growing old with their families, but they didn't know their habits were killing them. So listen closely. If you're hoping for a doctor with a gentle bedside manner, you won't find her here. A softly-softly approach doesn't work. I'm not a doctor who pulls her punches. All the people I met for the Turn Back Your Body Clock television series were told about their lifestyle shortcomings in no uncertain terms. It's my very own brand of tough love. But, to counter the bad news, I also told them exactly what they could do to add years to their lives. And in this book you'll find all the information you need to help you turn your life around and add years on to your own death age.

You're never too young to start thinking about your future. After all, your future may not be as long as you think. Perhaps you're a bright young thing in your twenties – the future looks rosy, and your life is one big party. But some day, and it may be sooner than you expect, your lifestyle may catch up with you.

If you are a housewife in your forties and think you live a sedate and 'safe' life except for that little smoking habit of yours, let me tell you you've got to start listening to your body and – most importantly – to your doctor. Don't leave it too late. Stop smoking. Stop vegetating. Start rolling back those years.

This book will enlighten you and guide you to a longer, healthier life. It's not all doom and gloom. Along with the other experts from the Turn Back Your Body Clock television series I have put together a hands-on, action-packed programme of what you can do – now! From getting to know your body and the warning signs that mean danger, to eating healthily and exercising, your life is in your hands. We'll help to make the advice real and practical. But you have it within your power to enjoy the life that you have now – and enjoy your old age, too.

Dr Una Coales

CHAPTER 1

HOW LONG HAVE YOU GOT?

30 questions that will change your life

Is your lifestyle knocking years off your lifespan? Try this quiz to find out. Add up the numbers in the brackets to find your score, and then start grabbing back some years by following the Turn Back Your Body Clock team's advice.

Lifestyle

1 Is the air polluted in the area where you live?
[2] Very (extensive industrial area)
[1] Average (urban area with some factories)
[0] No (rural/country area)

2 Have you ever smoked?
[4] Yes, until less than a year ago
[2] Yes, until less than 6 years ago
[0] No, I have never smoked

3 If you smoke, how many cigarettes do you smoke a day?
[3] 1–5
[4] 6–10
[5] 11–20
[6] More than 20

4 Are you exposed to second-hand smoke (whether or not you smoke yourself)?
[3] On a daily basis
[2] Several times a week
[1] Rarely

5 Do you drink alcohol in excess (that is, more than 21 units per week if you are a man, or 14 units per week if you are a woman)?
[4] Regularly
[2] Occasionally
[0] Never

6 Do you binge drink (more than 8 units in a session if you are a man, or more than 6 units in a session if you are a woman)?
[4] At least once a week
[2] At least once a month
[1] Occasionally
[0] Never

7 Do you have a close network of friends?
[0] Yes
[2] No

8 How often do you meet with friends or work colleagues socially?
[0] Once a week
[1] Once a fortnight
[2] Occasionally
[3] Never

9 How often do you visit or contact close family members?
[0] At least once a week
[1] At least once a fortnight
[2] Occasionally
[3] Never

10 Do you attend a church or similar, or undertake voluntary work?
[0] Regularly
[1] Occasionally (less than once a month)
[2] Never

Medical

11 Do you take advantage of the medical checks available from your doctor's surgery, such as mammograms, cervical smears and from 'well woman' and 'well man' clinics? (See pp. 185–6 for information on the tests available to you.)
[0] Yes
[3] No

12 What about your cholesterol level and blood pressure?
[0] I have them checked regularly, and they're fine
[3] I have them checked: one or both is too high, but I'm receiving treatment and advice from my doctor
[3] I haven't had them both checked

13 Do you floss your teeth?
[0] At least once a day
[1] Sometimes
[2] Never

14 Do you sunbathe or use a sunbed?
[4] At least once a week
[3] More than once a month
[2] Less than once a month
[0] Never

15 How would you describe your current stress level?
[0] Low
[1] Medium
[2] High

16 How well do you cope with stress?
[0] Stress helps get me motivated
[1] Reasonably well, I use techniques to help
[3] Badly, I feel constantly weighed down by stress

17 Do you engage in unprotected sex?
[4] Often
[3] Occasionally
[0] Never

18 Do you take substances classified as illegal drugs, or abuse prescription drugs or over-the-counter medicines?
[4] Often
[3] Rarely
[0] Never

Exercise and physique

19 Do you do any resistance exercise (also called strength training), such as going to a gym or using weights at home?

[0] At least once a week

[1] At least once a month

[2] Occasionally

[3] Never

20 How often do you do cardiovascular exercise that gets you out of breath, such as power walking, jogging, running, cycling or rowing for 20 minutes or more at a time?

[0] Twice a week or more

[1] Once a week

[2] Less than once a week

[3] Hardly ever

21 Do you do the recommended 30 minutes of moderate activity each day?

[0] Always

[2] Sometimes (3 times a week or less)

[3] Never

22 What is your Body Mass Index? (See p. 37 to learn how to work this out.)

[1] Below 18.5 (underweight)

[0] 18.5–24.9 (recommended)

[1] 25–29.9 (overweight)

[2] 30+ (obese)

23 What is your waist measurement?

[0] Less than 36 inches (90cm) for men, or 32 inches (80cm) for women

[1] 36–40 inches (90cm–100cm) for men, or 32–35 inches (80cm–88cm) for women

[3] Over 40 inches (100cm) for men, or 35 inches (88cm) for women

Nutrition

24 How many portions of processed meat or fast foods do you eat in a week?

[0] None

[1] 1–3

[2] Over 4

25 How often do you eat fatty, sugary or salty snacks in a week (crisps, chips, biscuits, cakes, chocolate bars, etc.)?

[0]   Never

[1]   Less than 3 times

[2]   4–7 times

[3]   More than 8 times

26 How many cans (or equivalent) of fizzy drink do you drink in a week?

[0]   2 or less

[1]   3–6

[2]   7 or more

27 How much water do you drink each day?

[2]   Less than 1 litre

[1]   1–1.5 litres

[0]   1.5 litres or more

28 How many portions of red meat do you eat in a week?

[0]   None

[1]   1–2 portions

[2]   More than 3 portions

29 How often do you eat your recommended 5-a-day portions of fruit and vegetables?

[0]   Every day

[1]   Less than 3 times a week

[2]   Less than 5 times a week

[3]   I never eat 5 portions of fruit and vegetables in a day

30 How often do you eat wholemeal or 'brown' products (brown rice, pasta, etc.)?

[0]   Always
[1]   Occasionally
[2]   Never

Now add up your score:

1–15: Well done! You're doing a lot to ensure you live to a ripe old age. But there's always room for improvement, so don't get complacent or you could start to knock years off your death age.

16–35: You try to live healthily, but some areas of your lifestyle let you down. Perhaps you smoke or have a weakness for takeaways and this is putting your health and your potential for a long, healthy life at risk. Be proud of your achievements, and tackle your problem areas straight away.

36–65: You are lopping years off your lifespan. You need to take yourself in hand and give your lifestyle a radical overhaul – now.

Over 65: Oh dear! It looks as though you could be eating, drinking, smoking or slouching – or a disastrous combination of all four – your way to an early grave. But don't despair. The worse your lifestyle is now, the greater its potential for improvement. The more years you can add to your death age.

Dr Una's top 10 bad habits

1 Smoking
2 Excessive drinking
3 Not taking enough exercise
4 Sunbathing
5 Not eating enough fruit and vegetables
6 Eating too many saturated and trans fats
7 Eating too much salt
8 Eating too much sugar
9 Not eating enough fibre
10 Not drinking enough water

CHAPTER 2

HOW TO
LIVE LONGER

the 12-point plan

How old are you? Easy question? Well, yes and no. You may know your calendar age, but what about your visual age, and – more importantly – your biological age.

Perhaps you were born 45 years ago. You may be one of those lucky people who look younger than their years. Or your lifestyle may have taken its toll on your looks. Your visual age may fool people into thinking that you're younger or older than you are.

But what about that all-important biological age? You may be in your forties and looking pretty good. But under the surface the picture could be less rosy. Your bones could be thinning, your arteries clogging, your lungs polluted with tobacco, your muscles wasting away through lack of use, your brain cells' connections withering away from lack of stimulation.

And you don't feel a thing … yet.

Your lifestyle could take years off your life, and reduce your quality of life for the years you do have. By the same token, giving your lifestyle a healthy overhaul can halt the damage in its tracks and even turn back the clock, effectively adding years to your life. It's never too late to change – and whatever changes you make, however small, it's all progress.

A lot of the process of ageing and some of your risk of chronic diseases such as heart disease and cancer is down to your genes (see p. 24 for more information on genetics). But your environment and lifestyle are still crucial, so there's a lot you can do to help yourself live longer and make sure those extra years are healthy and contented.

Just follow our plan and instantly you'll be putting less stress on your body and slowing down the ageing process. Some of these changes may be difficult. But don't forget that even small changes add up. When you're dealing with something as precious as your body, and your life, every bit of effort is worth it. Once you start caring for your body in the way it deserves you'll begin to feel better, and that's a huge motivator.

Let the 12-point plan be a springboard to the rest of the book. It tells you the changes you can make in order to put years on to your death age. Those changes will give you an in-depth knowledge that will help you to live healthily, eat well, give up the bad habits that can take years off your life and take up the good habits that could extend it by years.

This book will arm you with the knowledge to live longer, backed up with the practical advice you need to make it a reality. It will provide you with the healthy eating and exercise plans devised by the Turn Back Your Body Clock team – fitness expert Tim Bean and nutritionist Carina Norris. They helped the eight programme participants add years to their lives. Now you can do the same.

The 12 points that will change your life

1   STOP SMOKING

2   MAINTAIN A HEALTHY WEIGHT

3   TAKE REGULAR AEROBIC EXERCISE

4   DO STRENGTH TRAINING

5   CUT DOWN ON CONVENIENCE FOOD

6   INCREASE YOUR INTAKE OF FRUIT
      AND VEGETABLES

7   EAT THE RIGHT AMOUNT OF THE
      RIGHT FATS

8   FILL UP WITH STARCHY CARBOHYDRATES

9   INCREASE PULSES – DECREASE RED MEAT

10   EAT LESS SALT AND SUGAR

11   DRINK ALCOHOL ONLY IN MODERATION

12   REDUCE STRESS

Actioning the 12-point plan

You'll be launching a three-pronged attack on the life-sappers that can sabotage your chances of living a long and healthy life.

■ **Diet** – your diet affects every organ in your body. Poor diet has now overtaken smoking as the main drain on the NHS

■ **Exercise** – people who exercise have been proven to live longer

■ **Poor lifestyle choices** – smoking and drinking, for example, increase your risk of a variety of fatal diseases

If your lifestyle has aged you before your time, we'll help you to grab back those years and, if you can get your biological age below your calendar age, even add years to your life.

Your new, healthy lifestyle will also make you feel better, with higher energy levels, fewer minor illnesses, less aches and pains and a more relaxed attitude to life.

Think of it this way. As well as adding years to your life, you'll also be adding life to your years.

1 Stop smoking

■ Quitting is one of the most important things you can do to extend your life.

  ■ *WHY?* Smoking is a major cause of lung cancer (as well as other cancers), heart attacks and stroke

2 Maintain a healthy weight

■ Obesity can kill you in many ways.

  ■ *WHY?* It increases your risk of a whole host of diseases, including heart disease, stroke, several cancers and Type 2 diabetes. It also makes things much more risky if you have to undergo surgery

  ■ Excess weight also leads to increased wear and tear on the joints, increasing the risk of osteoarthritis

  ■ Less well known is the fact that being underweight isn't healthy either. To find out what weight you should be see p. 37

Quitting is one of the most important things you can do to extend your life

3 Take regular aerobic exercise

■ We need aerobic exercise (also called 'cardio') – the kind that gets our lungs working and our hearts pumping.

   ■ *WHY?* To keep our cardiovascular system in shape
   ■ Even a little aerobic exercise – for example a brisk daily walk – can reduce our risk of chronic diseases such as heart disease and cancer. It also burns calories, helping us to maintain a healthy weight
   ■ Weight-bearing aerobic exercise, such as walking, running or jogging, also helps strengthen and maintain our bones, reducing the risk of the bone-thinning disease osteoporosis

4 Do strength training

■ Strength, or resistance exercise, involves working with weights – either machines at a gym, or hand-held weights, or even the weight of your own body (as in push-ups).

   ■ *WHY?* It builds and maintains muscle, helping to prevent the loss of muscle associated with ageing and increasing our metabolic rate and 'fat-burning' ability
   ■ Weight-bearing strength exercises also reduce the risk of osteoporosis

5 Cut down on convenience food

■ Make as much of your own food as you can.

   ■ *WHY?* Processed foods are often full of unhealthy ingredients, such as saturated and trans fats, sugar, salt and artificial additives. You'll also know exactly what goes into your meals.

6 Increase your intake of fruit and vegetables

■ Fruit and vegetables could be your best dietary medicine against the big killers – cancer and cardiovascular disease (heart attack and stroke).

   ■ *WHY?* They're packed with vitamins and minerals and antioxidants that support the immune system, making you less vulnerable to disease and infection. They're also a great source of fibre, which helps prevent digestive disorders. One type of fibre – the so-called soluble fibre found particularly in oats – also lowers the risk of heart disease by helping to control your cholesterol level

Set yourself goals

Don't be daunted by the 12 points – set yourself goals,
both short- and long-term. For example:

Short-term goals

■ *Cut down from two sugars in your tea or coffee to one*

■ *Buy yourself an exercise journal and start using it*

■ *Enrol in a yoga class*

Long-term goals

■ *Slim down to a weight that is healthy for you by this time next
year; give yourself longer if you have a lot of pounds to shed*

■ *Get fit enough to take part in a fun run for your favourite charity*

■ *Give up smoking*

Short-term goals shouldn't be too ambitious but, because you can
achieve them relatively quickly, you'll feel you're getting somewhere.

Long-term goals are bigger in scope and you need to give yourself
longer to reach them. It's easier, too, if you break them down into
mini goals, for example giving yourself a weight-loss target every
two months.

Reward yourself when you reach a target – how about buying
yourself some new exercise gear?

- It's recommended that you eat at least five portions of fruit and vegetables per day, but few of us manage this many
- And if five is good, then more is better! Aim for at least three fruit and three vegetable portions per day

7 Eat the right amount of the right fats

- Fats are high in calories and can lead to you piling on the pounds.
    - *WHY?* Gram for gram, fats are more than twice as calorific as protein and carbohydrates. Fat also enhances the taste of food, making you more likely to eat more than you should
    - You need to keep an eye on your total fat intake and cut down if you need to lose weight
- Some fats are bad for you, others are good.
    - *WHY?* Saturated and trans fats increase our risk of heart disease, while mono-unsaturated and poly-unsaturated fats can help lower it
    - Reduce your intake of saturated fats (found mainly in animal products such as meat, chicken, eggs and dairy products) and trans fats (found mainly in processed foods). But ensure that you get enough of the 'good' fats in your diet – these are the mono-unsaturated and poly-unsaturated fats (including the Omega-3s and Omega-6s). Unsaturated fats are good for your heart and also help to balance moods

8 Fill up with starchy carbohydrates

- So-called 'complex' carbohydrates – the starchy ones such as bread, pasta, potatoes, rice and other cereals – are an excellent source of sustained energy.
    - *WHY?* 'Simple' or sugary carbohydrates produce a hit of energy, but little else except trouble. Complex carbohydrates, by contrast, provide a 'slow' source of fuel, keeping our blood sugar levels nice and steady, and keeping us going between meals so that we're less likely to reach for a sugary snack

9 Increase pulses – decrease red meat

- Increasing the amount of pulses (beans and lentils) in your diet, while decreasing the amount of red meat, can cut your risk of obesity, heart disease and cancer.
    - *WHY?* We need to ensure that we get a good supply of protein,

without taking in too much unhealthy fat. Red meat is a great source of protein and iron, but it's also high in saturated fat
- *WHY?* Beans and lentils have the added benefit of being packed with fibre, slow release energy and healthy phytochemicals

10 Eat less salt and sugar

- Salt and sugar are not good for you.
  - *WHY?* Sugar is calorific and, because of the way it gives you a quick hit of energy then leaves you craving another sugary snack, can lead to weight gain. It can also play havoc with the state of your teeth
  - *WHY?* Salt can raise your blood pressure, predisposing you to heart disease and stroke. It's also implicated in an increased risk of stomach cancer
  - *WHY?* Both make foods taste good, and because many of our calorific 'comfort foods' are packed with them they can contribute to weight gain

11 Drink alcohol only in moderation

- An alarming number of people are unaware that their drinking is affecting their chances of living a long, healthy life.
  - *WHY?* Although a small amount of alcohol (especially red wine) is thought to have some health benefits, drinking more than this is positively dangerous. Too much alcohol causes liver damage and increases your risk of heart disease, Type 2 diabetes and certain cancers

12 Reduce stress

- Stress is implicated in a variety of illnesses.
  - *WHY?* It suppresses the immune system, making you more vulnerable to infections and cancers. It also raises your blood pressure and slows the healing process when you're injured
  - Reducing the stress in your life – and learning to cope with the stress you can't avoid – helps you to enjoy life and feel younger

genetics

How long you live depends mainly on three things:
- **Your behaviour and lifestyle choices:** what you eat, how much exercise you take and whether you smoke or drink, etc.
- **Genetics:** the biological resources you're born with
- **Accidents** and other elements beyond your control

You can do a lot to ensure that your choices are healthy ones that promote a long life, and you can go a long way to avoid accidents. But genetics are involved too – the genes you inherit from your parents also determine how long you live.

- **'Longevity genes'.** Scientists have discovered large numbers of genes that act together in complex ways to determine your 'natural' death age – that is, how long you'd live without taking into consideration any of the other factors like behaviour and chance

- **'Disease' genes.** You can also inherit genes that cause certain diseases, or make you more likely to develop them

Examples of genetic diseases include:

- Huntington's disease
- Cystic fibrosis
- Sickle cell anaemia
- Haemophilia

It is often said that some diseases, such as certain cancers, 'run in the family'. It doesn't mean you'll definitely get the disease, just that it's more important for you to be regularly checked for that disease, and to make the lifestyle choices that minimise your risk. Diseases where genes play a part in how susceptible you are include:

- Breast cancer
- Colon cancer
- Heart disease

vitamins and minerals

If you're deficient in micronutrients – vitamins and minerals – your health suffers. Sometimes the effect is obvious. Vitamin A deficiency, for example, can make your skin dry and flaky. But the effect can also be more subtle and sinister. Long-term deficiencies – even low-grade deficiencies – can suppress your immune system, making you more likely to pick up infections and less able to shake them off. They can also increase your risk of chronic diseases such as heart disease and cancer.

In an ideal world you would eat a fantastic nutritious diet containing all the vital vitamins and marvellous minerals you need. But the real world is full of demands that prevent you from eating all the foods you should, as well as nutrient-sappers that stop your body from absorbing and using the micronutrients you do eat.

■ Smoking depletes vitamin C stores, so if you're a smoker you need extra vitamin C in your diet. Smoking runs down levels of B vitamins too, so it's particularly important for smokers to get plenty of B vitamin-rich foods such as meat, dairy, wholegrains and pulses

■ Stress also uses up extra B vitamins, so you need more when you're under pressure

■ If you're a heavy drinker you face a double-whammy when it comes to B vitamins. Not only are you less able to absorb them, but alcohol also depletes the body's levels of these vitamins

■ Vegetarians and vegans will find it hard to get enough vitamin B12, because it's only found naturally in animal products

■ The main source of vitamin D is a chemical reaction triggered by sunlight on the skin. In a country with a grey climate, people with dark skin may be deficient in vitamin D as the pigment in the skin absorbs some of the relatively weak sunlight before it can be used to make vitamin D. Those who don't get out into the sun much, such as the elderly or housebound, may also be deficient

What vitamins do you need, and where can you find them?

Vitamin	Function	Animal sources	Non-meat sources
Vitamin A	Healthy vision and skin, also supports the immune system	Liver, oily fish, milk and eggs	Spinach, broccoli, plus yellow and orange foods, such as carrots, sweet potato, peaches and apricots
B Vitamins (Vitamins B1, B2, B3, B6, B12)	Energy release from food, production of healthy blood cells, maintenance of a healthy nervous system	Meat, fish, dairy products, eggs	Wholegrains, beans and lentils, nuts, seeds and vegetables
Vitamin C	Supports the immune system, promotes healing, enhances absorption of iron from the diet		Fruit (especially kiwi fruit, blackcurrants, strawberries, citrus fruits), yellow and red peppers, Brussels sprouts
Vitamin D	Vital for healthy bones and teeth, as it helps the body absorb and use calcium. Helps prevent osteoporosis	Oily fish, meat, eggs, dairy products	Sunlight on the skin

Vitamin	Function	Animal sources	Non-meat sources
Vitamin E	Supports the immune system, protects from infection, needed for healthy blood vessels		Wheatgerm, nuts and seeds and their oils, wholemeal bread, avocado, spinach
Folic Acid	Needed for effective absorption of nutrients, and prevention of anaemia. May also reduce the risk of heart disease	Liver, eggs	Green leafy vegetables, brown rice, beans and lentils, wheatgerm

Mineral	Function	Animal sources	Non-animal sources
Iron	Production of healthy red blood cells and prevention of anaemia	Red meat (especially liver)	Beans and lentils, green vegetables, dried fruit (especially apricots)
Calcium	Maintenance of healthy bones and teeth, and prevention of osteoporosis	Dairy foods, tinned fish where the bones are eaten (e.g. salmon and sardines)	Tofu, kale and other green leafy vegetables
Zinc	Supporting the immune system, healthy skin	Oysters, meat, fish, chicken, eggs, dairy products	Green leafy vegetables, beans and lentils

Supplements vs real food

High doses of vitamins have had a good press, with reports claiming amazing health benefits such as preventing and curing a whole host of killer diseases from cancer to heart disease.

But do they work, and are they safe?

The research is certainly exciting. But many health professionals are concerned about the conflicting results being found by scientific studies – one study shows a vitamin prevents cancer, then another says it doesn't – or even increases your risk of contracting cancer.

Some of these vitamins can be toxic in high doses. They accumulate in the body and we don't yet know enough about the long-term effects of supplementation.

For the time being at least, it is far better – and safer – to get your vitamins and minerals from real food. It's virtually impossible to overdose on vitamins found in food (although pregnant women should avoid liver because its high vitamin A content is potentially harmful to a foetus). Also, the micronutrients in real food interact in helpful ways we're only just beginning to unravel – and these benefits cannot yet be bottled!

However, there are some exceptions to the 'food not pills' ethos. If you're planning a baby you should take a 400 micrograms folic acid supplement for at least four weeks before conception and the first three months of pregnancy. Pregnant women can also benefit from a multivitamin specially tailored to cope with the increased nutritional demands placed on their bodies by a developing baby. Ask your doctor or midwife for advice.

Vegans may be deficient in vitamin B12 and might benefit from a general B vitamin supplement, or a good quality (but not megadose) multivitamin. But you should ask a qualified nutritionist or dietician for advice rather than just picking up a bottle you like the look of.

If you're worried, a good quality multivitamin and mineral won't hurt you and could prove a helpful 'safety net' if any micronutrients are temporarily lacking from your diet.

are your children a dietary time bomb?

Could we be raising a generation of children who will die before their parents?

Many of today's children are eating diets saturated with fat, sugar, salt and artificial chemicals. They are missing out on healthy foods such as fruit and vegetables, and slicing years off their adult lives in the process. They are also far less active than their parents were – tending to be ferried everywhere by car and often preferring to slouch in front of the TV or a computer screen rather than burn off energy taking part in sports.

Conditions such as obesity, high blood pressure, clogged arteries and Type 2 diabetes (previously called 'adult onset diabetes') are being found in teenagers and even children. Once, these diseases didn't show up until people hit their forties, but because children are picking up self-destructive eating habits, they're giving themselves a head start in damaging their bodies.

Childhood obesity, especially excess weight around the stomach, has been proven to be a key factor of the Metabolic Syndrome – a group of symptoms that is associated with Type 2 diabetes and an increased risk of heart disease and stroke in adulthood.

This generation of kids could be heading for heart attacks and strokes in their forties rather than their sixties. Now that is a national disaster.

The culprits

Fat Burgers, chips, pizzas, sausages and crisps – so many of the foods children love are dripping with fat. Processed meat products are high in saturated fats, the kind that raise levels of harmful cholesterol and increase the risk of cancer. And all fat contributes to obesity.

Sugar Children love sweet things. Sugar (especially between meals) can rot their teeth and because it's so 'more-ish', sugary foods and fizzy drinks can lead to piling on the pounds. Children filling up on sweets and chocolates are also less likely to eat healthy foods such as fruit and vegetables – the very foods that could add years to their lives.

Salt Processed foods and snacks such as crisps can be amazingly high in salt, and while an adult's recommended maximum salt intake is 6g per day, a child's safe maximum is proportionally smaller. And salty diets in childhood can lead to the problems associated with high blood pressure – mainly heart disease and stroke – striking that much earlier. These are the recommended daily maximums:

- 1–3 years old: 2g salt per day (0.8g sodium)
- 4–6 years old: 3g salt per day (1.2g sodium)
- 7–10 years old: 5g salt per day (2g sodium)
- 11 years old and over, as adults: 6g salt per day (2.5g sodium)

Additives Think how many of the foods aimed at children are brightly coloured. Although additives used in food have to undergo testing for toxicity, there's still widespread concern about whether the 'safe levels' set could still be harmful over the long term, especially by increasing cancer risk. And when you think about it, it makes sense to minimise your intake of unnecessary artificial chemicals, if there's even just a possibility they could be harming you.

The most recent National Diet and Nutrition Survey of British children aged 4–18 found that they ate more than the recommended levels of sugar, salt and fat (including saturated fat), and not enough fibre, vitamins and minerals.
- *The most commonly eaten foods were white bread, savoury snacks, biscuits, chips, other potatoes and chocolate*
- *The meats most commonly eaten were chicken and turkey*
- *The most popular fruits were apples and pears, followed by bananas*
- *Three-quarters of the children drank 'regular' fizzy drinks in the week they were surveyed, and 45% drank 'diet' fizzy drinks*
- *Fizzy drinks were the main source of sugar in the children's diet, followed by chocolate*
- *Salt intake – not even including salt added at the table – was more than double the RNI, or recommended nutrient intake*
- *8% of boys and 11% of girls had blood cholesterol levels higher than recommended*

CHILDREN'S FOOD: How to live longer

Parents are the biggest influence on a child's food preferences, so from an early age get them into the habit of eating nutritious foods. Eating habits established in childhood can last a lifetime.

- Set a good example – you won't be able to persuade them to eat their veggies if you slob in front of the TV with a pizza

- Don't give up if a child initially turns up their nose at the healthy food you offer. Studies have shown that it can take up to 10 tries before a child decides they like a new food. Persistence pays in the end

- Don't ban 'unhealthy' foods completely. Your children will only rebel and buy them themselves when you're not there

- Explain why junk food is just that – junk – and why smart kids don't eat it

Things you can do – NOW!

- *Have a healthy 'snack box' at home. Rather than chocolate and biscuits, fill it with snack-size bags of dried fruit and unsalted nuts, or home-made treats such as low-sugar and low-fat oat bars*

- *Keep the fruit bowl overflowing, and encourage them to grab from it when they feel a snack attack coming on*

- *Encourage children when they show an interest in sports, and steer them towards 'active' toys like bikes, skipping ropes, hula hoops and space hoppers*

- *Be an active family – make fun walks, family cycle rides and kick-about football in the park part of your weekend treats*

- *Children learn by example, so take up a sport yourself and let your enthusiasm rub off on them. Many adult sports clubs have junior sections*

- *If it's practical, leave the car at home and walk to school and to the shops with them*

CHAPTER 3

FIGHTING THE FLAB

obesity

The scientific definition of obesity is having a Body Mass Index (BMI) of more than 30 (see p. 37 for how to work out your BMI). Obesity is now such a widespread and serious health problem that the World Health Organisation (WHO) is calling it an epidemic. Being overweight or obese (extremely overweight) is expected to cut the average life expectancy in the United States by 5 years within the next 50 years, and the UK is thought to be just a few years behind.

While more men than women are overweight, a greater proportion of women than men fall into the more serious obese category.

mythbuster

The Myth: *Dairy foods make you fat.*

The Truth: Some dairy foods – like butter, cream, full-fat cheeses and milk – are high in fat. But dairy products are a great source of calcium. If you choose low-fat versions, dairy could be good for your waistline. Scientists have found that getting enough calcium can help prevent weight gain.

Being overweight, particularly if you're unfit as well, seriously increases your risk of several life-threatening diseases and can take years off your life expectancy.

If you're overweight or obese you're more prone to:
- High blood pressure
- Increased blood cholesterol
- Coronary heart disease
- Stroke
- Type 2 diabetes
- Certain cancers, such as uterus, breast, bowel and kidney cancer
- Dementia. An American study, reported in the *British Medical Journal*, found that being overweight or obese significantly increased the risk of degenerative brain diseases like Alzheimer's
- Kidney failure
- Eye diseases, such as age-related macular degeneration, glaucoma and cataracts

Being overweight also increases your risk of complications, and even death, during surgery. It puts extra strain on your joints, intensifying everyday aches and pains, and making you more susceptible to osteoarthritis. It can even wreck your chances of having children because obesity messes up the male hormone system responsible for sperm production, as well as making it more difficult for women to conceive.

Scientists talk about our 'obesogenic environment'. In a nutshell, the world we live in makes it easy for us to put on weight. Most of us are cash-richer and time-poorer than ever before. Food manufacturers, supermarkets and fast-food restaurants ply us with a huge, tempting array of convenience foods (many of them very high in fat and sugar), and that's before the multi-million-pound advertising industry puts its oar in.

Add to that the fact that far more of us than ever before have cars and drive everywhere, have desk jobs, and that our hobbies tend to be more concerned with relaxing, unwinding and socialising than any form of serious activity – and it's easy to recognise a recipe for disaster.

Why do I put on weight?

It's not rocket science.

If energy (calories) in = energy out, you maintain your weight.

If you eat more calories than you use up, you store them, and put on weight.

If you burn more calories (through activity) than you take in, you lose weight.

It's as simple as that.

Some people have a genetic advantage or disadvantage. At the extremes of the scale there are the human dustbins with turbo-charged metabolisms, who seem able to eat what they like without ever getting fat. And then there are those who say they only need to look at a cake to put on a stone.

Also, some people have naturally bigger appetites, so they're more likely to overeat.

But when all is said and done, you have to sort out your 'energy in vs energy out' equation. Don't eat more calories than your body needs.

mythbuster

The Myth: *I can't help it – it's my genes' fault!*

The Truth: Except in the case of a few specific medical conditions, genes can only increase your *risk* of putting on weight. Only *you* can actually make yourself fat.

OBESITY: Vital statistics

- A report by the National Audit Office (2001) stated that deaths linked to obesity shorten lifespan by an average of 9 years
- Obesity in England trebled between 1980 and 2005
- 50% of adults in the UK are overweight, and 15–20% are obese
- 15% of children in the UK are overweight, and a further 16% are obese – that's 31% of children who are too heavy
- Obesity is responsible for 18 million sick days per year
- Obesity is also linked to 30,000 deaths per year, resulting in 40,000 lost years of working life

OBESITY: How to live longer

Remember the 12-point plan? All 12 points will help keep your weight in check. But to start you on your way, here are some quick fixes to help you think about changing the way you eat.

Start to cut down the amount of processed foods you consume. When you increase the amount of home-made food you eat and cut out the convenience foods, your fat and sugar intake will plummet

Avoid fast-food restaurants and takeaways. Most of the options on offer are laden with calories

Watch out for hidden sugars. Many breakfast cereals and tinned products, such as beans and spaghetti, are full of them. And many foods promoted as 'low fat' are less than slimming because of the amount of sugar they contain

Eat only when you're hungry, not because you're bored, upset or out of habit. If you must have a chocolate or a biscuit, take just one and put the packet away. Packets of biscuits and chocolates left open can be too tempting to resist and, before you realise it, the packet's empty

Things to do – NOW!

■ Increase your incidental activity. Exercise doesn't have to involve sports or classes – increase the amount of energy you use in everyday activities. If it's not too far, walk or cycle to work. Otherwise, get off the bus one stop earlier or park the car further away, and walk the rest of the way. Take the stairs rather than the lift at work and when shopping. At home, run up the stairs rather than walking. Walk the dog – or take him for a jog. When you're gardening or doing housework, give it an extra bit of welly

■ Fidget more. Scientists have found that natural fidgeters use up more calories than other people. So take a leaf out of their book and become one of those people who can never sit still. Get up to change the TV channel, and when something needs taking upstairs do it immediately rather than waiting for a heap of things to accumulate on the bottom step

■ Introduce exercise into your routine. Find sports and activities you enjoy, and make them a habit. (See pp. 168–72 for the Turn Back Your Body Clock 8-Week

Keep a grip on reality Even if you're desperate to lose weight, don't get obsessed with counting calories. They're useful when you want to compare two products on the supermarket shelf, but you've got better things to do with your time than add up the kcals in everything you eat and drink. It can also lead to an unhealthy pre-occupation with 'dieting' as opposed to a healthy diet.

Far better to go by the general rules and guidelines offered here – such as eating slightly smaller portions, less processed food, less fat, less sugar, more wholefoods and more fruit and vegetables.

Help from your GP Your doctor could prescribe a drug (called Xenical or Orlistat) to treat obesity. But its use is carefully regulated and you first have to be able to prove that you've been able to lose some weight 'on your own'. The drugs work by stopping your body from absorbing some of the fat from your food. That grease has to go somewhere, so the main side effect is oily bowel movements. Still, if the alternative is an early death from an obesity-related cause, it's probably worth it. There's also an appetite suppressant called sibutramine available from your doctor.

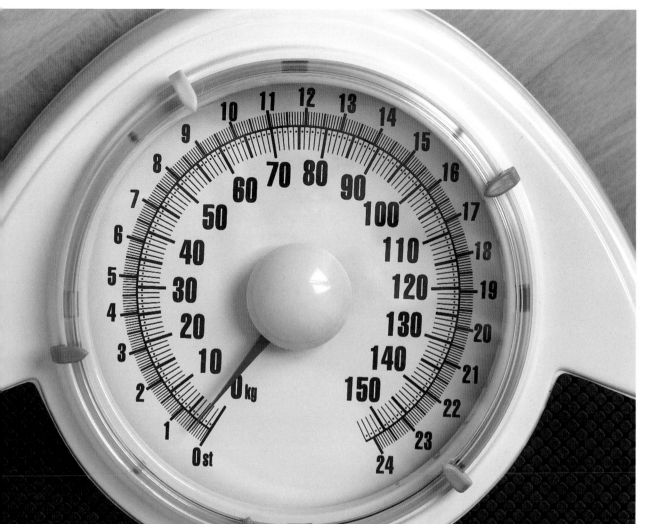

how much should I weigh?

The method usually used to determine whether you're overweight is the Body Mass Index, or BMI. This tells you how heavy you are for your height.

BMI = your weight (in kg) divided by your height (in metres) squared.

So, for a woman weighing 57kg (approximately 9 stone) who is 1.63m (5'4") tall:

57kg divided by (1.63 x 1.63) = BMI of 21.4

- ■ Below 18.5 = underweight
- ■ 18.6 to 24.9 = healthy weight
- ■ 25 to 29.9 = overweight
- ■ 30 and over = obese

But there's a problem with BMI. It measures whether you're overweight but not whether you're overfat, and being fat is the real danger. BMI doesn't take into account the amount of muscle you're carrying. And because muscle is heavier than fat, well-muscled people like professional sportsmen and sportswomen and bodybuilders have BMIs that class them as obese when they're not fat or unhealthy.

Although BMI is still useful, there are two better ways of determining 'fatness': body fat percentage, and waist-to-hip ratio.

Body fat percentage

This takes into account how much of your bulk is actually fat. It's generally measured using special scales that you can buy or find at your GP's surgery or your gym, or hand-held monitoring devices. There aren't official figures for what's a healthy 'fatness', so the figures below are a guide.

	Male	Female
Underfat	Under 13%	Under 21%
Healthy	13–18%	21–25%
Overfat	18–25%	25–31%
Obese	Over 26%	Over 31%

Waist-to-hip ratio

Are you an apple or a pear? Being an 'apple' who stores fat around the waist can take years off your life. Being a 'pear' who collects weight on the bottom and thighs is less risky. Fat stored around the waist is more likely to 'escape' into the bloodstream, contributing to high blood cholesterol. Apple-shaped people, with so-called 'central obesity', face a higher risk of:

- Heart disease
- Stroke
- Type 2 diabetes
- High blood pressure
- Certain cancers

There's not a lot you can do about where your body stores fat – it's mostly down to your genes. Men generally take after their fathers where fat storage is concerned, and women their mothers.

And as a general rule, men are more likely to be apple shaped while most women tend towards pear shaped.

It's not possible to remove fat just from your tummy. But if you fall into the apple-shaped category, it's more important for you to watch your weight and shed some pounds in order to get your waist down to a safe measurement.

You should also minimise your intake of harmful saturated and trans fats, while making sure you have enough of the 'good' unsaturated fats. (See pp. 41–3 for more information on fats.)

Measure your middle

Waist measurement danger level:
- *Larger than 100cm / 40 inches for men*
- *Larger than 88cm / 35 inches for women*

Your waist-to-hip measurement ratio is another useful guide – take your waist measurement, and divide it by your hip measurement.

Waist-to-hip ratio danger level:
- *Ratio over 0.9 for men*
- *Ratio over 0.85 for women*

If your waist-to-hip ratio is over 0.9 for men (0.85 for women), your health becomes more vulnerable because fat stored around the waist is more likely to contribute to high blood lipid and cholesterol levels, with an increased risk of clogging of the arteries and heart problems.

How much fat?

Recommended daily fat intakes for an average man or woman (74kg man, 60kg woman):

Total fat intake – maximum
- *99g for average man*
- *75g for average woman*

Saturated fat intake – maximum
- *28g for average man*
- *21g for average woman*

Recommended mono-unsaturated fat intake
- *34g for average man*
- *25g for average woman*

Recommended poly-unsaturated fat intake
- *17g for average man*
- *13g for average woman*

Recommended Omega-3 intake – minimum
- *3.4g for average man*
- *2.6g for average woman*

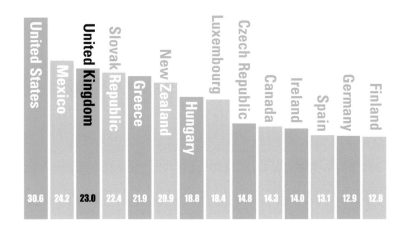

United States	Mexico	United Kingdom	Slovak Republic	Greece	New Zealand	Hungary	Luxembourg	Czech Republic	Canada	Ireland	Spain	Germany	Finland
30.6	24.2	23.0	22.4	21.9	20.9	18.8		18.4	14.8	14.3	14.0	13.1	12.9	12.8

Obesity around the world as a percentage of adult population

Copyright OECD HEALTH DATA 2005, October 05

know your fats

Eating too much fat, especially if it's the wrong sort, can knock years off your life. Fats are packed with calories (9 calories per gram, which is more than twice that found in carbohydrates or protein), so if your diet is high in fat it's all too easy to put on weight. And that's not all…

Eating too much fat can lead to:

- High cholesterol levels
- Heart disease
- Stroke
- Diabetes
- High blood pressure
- An increased risk of certain cancers

Turn to 'How much fat?' (p. 39) to see the amount of fat you're allowed in a healthy, balanced 'maintenance' diet. But beware hidden fats! Your fat intake soon mounts up when you remember that it's not just what you spread on your toast and fry your food in. Fat also lurks in lean-looking meat, in milk and other dairy products, in eggs and, of course, all those processed ready meals and fast foods.

Getting the balance right

And it's not just the total amount of fat you eat that's important – the balance of the different kinds of fat matters too.

You do need a certain amount of fat in your diet (though admittedly it's less than most of us eat), and it's important to try to make as much of your intake as possible the good 'protective' kind of fat, rather than the harmful kind.

good fats, bad fats

You need to know your enemy – and your friend. There are four main kinds of fats (fatty acids), all with different health hazards and benefits. Once you know what you're dealing with, you can make the food choices that can considerably increase your death age.

Saturated fats

These are the fats we need to cut down on. They don't just help make you fat – they can lop years off your lifespan by contributing to a variety of diseases and health problems.

- Overweight and obesity
- High blood pressure
- Clogged arteries (atherosclerosis)
- Cardiovascular disease (heart disease and stroke)
- Type 2 diabetes
- Several cancers, including breast cancer and colon cancer

Saturated fats include the fat in animal products such as meat, poultry, eggs and dairy products, as well as hard 'tropical oils' that are solid at room temperature, such as coconut oil and palm oil. Around 6 out of 7 adults in the UK eat more than the recommended amount of saturated fat.

Cut your saturated fat intake by:
- Lowering your intake of animal products – swap meat-based meals for those based on beans and lentils
- Substituting low-fat versions of dairy products such as milk, yoghurt and cheese for the full-cream varieties
- Putting low-fat fromage frais or quark (a soft, mild cheese, similar to fromage frais) on your desserts rather than cream
- Going for sorbet or yog-ice rather than ice cream
- Using a low-fat spread (high in mono-unsaturates and low in saturates) on your bread and toast. Spread it thinly!
- Not using spread on your bread when you're making a sandwich with a moist filling

Trans fats

If saturated fats are bad, trans fats are worse! The food manufacturing industry uses a chemical process to transform liquid vegetable oil into semi-solid gunk that finds its way into a huge range of products on our supermarket shelves. They're also used for frying in many fast-food restaurants.

Manufactured trans fats are unnatural or 'fake fats', named 'trans' because of their molecular structure, with a pair of hydrogen atoms on opposite sides of a double bond (trans as in across).

Why do the manufacturers love trans fats so much? Well, they're cheap, versatile, virtually tasteless and last for ages so they increase the shelf life of the products they go into.

■ Avoid trans fats where possible – read the labels, and avoid hydrogenated or partially hydrogenated vegetable oil, or shortening. You won't see 'trans fats' on the labels – sneaky, eh?
■ Watch out for trans fats in:
   ■ Ready meals
   ■ Instant soups and noodles
   ■ Cook-in sauces
   ■ Biscuits, pastries and cakes
   ■ Chocolates
   ■ Dessert and cake mixes
   ■ Ice creams

Now on to the 'good' fats.

Unsaturated fats

These are generally liquid at room temperature – in other words, they're oils. These are the fats that, eaten in moderation, protect us from cardiovascular disease that the 'bad' fats promote. And unsaturated fats even have some extra health benefits of their own.

There are two main kinds of unsaturated fats:

Mono-unsaturated fats These oils help lower your levels of 'bad' LDL cholesterol, while raising your levels of 'good' HDL cholesterol. (For more on types of cholesterol see p. 76.) Good examples of mono-unsaturated fats include olive oil, canola oil and peanut oil, as well as the oil found in avocados.

Poly-unsaturated fats These oils help lower your levels of 'bad' LDL cholesterol, while maintaining your levels of 'good' HDL cholesterol. There are two main kinds of poly-unsaturated fats:

Omega-3 fatty acids These are brilliant for heart health. They have a beneficial effect on our cholesterol levels and also make the blood less 'sticky' and therefore less likely to form life-threatening clots. Omega-3s are also good for your brain. Population studies have shown that countries with a high Omega-3 intake have particularly low levels of depression and less dementia in old age. These are also the oils that doctors are finding can produce dramatic benefits in children suffering from ADHD (Attention Deficit Hyperactivity Disorder). The scientific findings suggest that they could be important in smoothing your moods.

Omega-6 fatty acids These healthy oils have similar heart health effects to Omega-3s, but the benefits aren't quite so dramatic. They may also reduce our risk of Type 2 diabetes. Omega-6s are found in nuts and seeds, as well as some vegetable oils – corn oil, sunflower oil and safflower oil.

FATS: how to live longer

Get your fats right, and add years to your death age.

Cut down your total fat intake.
■ *Cut down on fried and processed foods*
■ *Cut down on biscuits, cakes and pastries*

Replace saturated fats with unsaturated fats.
■ *Replace meat protein with vegetarian protein (beans, lentils, etc)*
■ *Use a low-fat unsaturated fat spread, in small quantities*
■ *When you do fry foods, use olive oil*

Avoid trans fats.
■ *Read the food labels and avoid hydrogenated and partially hydrogenated vegetable fats*
■ *Avoid fast-food restaurants, unless they can guarantee that they don't fry in hydrogenated fats*

Eat plenty of fish, with at least two portions of oily fish per week to supply you with Omega-3s. The best sources of Omega-3s are tinned or fresh salmon, sardines, mackerel and fresh tuna. You can also get them from flax seeds (also called linseeds)

Things you can do – NOW!

- **Start eating more oily fish. The best sources of Omega-3s are oily fish such as salmon, mackerel, pilchards, sardines and fresh tuna. Note that the tuna canning process removes most of the Omega-3s**

- **If you're vegetarian, you can find much smaller amounts of Omega-3s in flax seeds (linseeds) and their oil, or you can buy a vegetarian Omega-3 supplement**

CHAPTER 4

VICES

alcohol

A drink with a meal, or socialising with friends, can enhance our lives, and moderate amounts of alcohol (especially red wine) might even reduce our risk of heart attacks. But excessive alcohol intake is associated with a whole host of health problems, many of which can subtract years from your life:

- Alcoholism
- Liver damage
- Impaired judgement and increased risk of accidents
- Weight gain and obesity
- Increased risk of liver, mouth, throat, voicebox and oesophagus cancers
- Increased risk of Type 2 diabetes
- Increased risk of heart disease, including heart rhythm disturbances
- Stomach problems
- Depression
- Dangerous interactions with prescription and other medicines
- Sexual and fertility problems

The Myth: *You have to get totally off your head for it to be classed as 'binge drinking'.*

The Truth: The official definition is anything over 6 units at a time for women, or 8 units at a time for men.

It can also cause insomnia and disturbed sleep by depleting serotonin, the chemical needed for sleep and mood regulation. It also depletes your body of nutrients, especially B vitamins – B6 and folic acid. And, thanks to dehydration, it will also give you a horrendous hangover if you overindulge.

Dr Una says...

From the moment it passes your lips, alcohol receives special treatment from the body. Because it does not need digesting, it can be absorbed straight from the stomach and into the bloodstream. When drunk on an empty stomach, alcohol can reach the brain in less than a minute.

Alcohol is a toxin, so it is sent straight to the liver for detoxifying. When the alcohol arrives, the liver has to stop what it is doing and immediately set to work dealing with the 'poison'.

But the liver can only break down about one unit of alcohol per hour, and any amount above this is turned away as it arrives and sent back into the bloodstream, causing damaging effects to all the cells it comes into contact with.

Alcohol distracts the liver from its other 499 functions. The main effect of this is the build-up of fatty substances in the liver that prevent it from functioning properly. So-called 'fatty liver' is the first stage of liver disease seen in heavy drinkers. It can be reversed if the drinking stops. But if you continue to drink, liver cells die and there is a progression to cirrhosis, which is irreversible.

One unit of alcohol is equivalent to:
- *Half a pint of average-strength beer, lager or cider (3–4% alcohol by volume)*
- *Small glass of wine (9% alcohol by volume)*
- *Standard pub measure (25 ml) of spirits (40% alcohol by volume)*
- *Standard pub measure (50 ml) of fortified wine, e.g. sherry, port (20% alcohol by volume)*

Remember that a lot of pubs and restaurants serve wine in large 175ml (2 unit) glasses, and most people drink pints of beer or lager, and double measures of spirits. 'Home measures' are also notoriously generous – it's not unusual for a whisky poured by a friend to be a double or triple pub measure.

ALCOHOL: Vital statistics

- Alcohol is implicated in over 6,500 deaths a year in England and Wales
- Since the 1970s, there has been an 8-fold increase in deaths from chronic liver disease among men aged 37–45, and a 7-fold increase among women of this age
- About 25% of alcohol-related deaths are due to accidents. 1 in 6 people attending accident and emergency departments for treatment is there because of alcohol-related injuries. This figure rises to 8 in 10 at the peak times of evenings and night-time
- Alcohol is implicated in 1 in 7 road accident deaths
- Alcohol-related problems cost the NHS £3 billion a year in hospital services
- In a survey, 29% of men and 17% of women had drunk more than the recommended safe amount in the previous week
- 1 in 4 adults in the UK admit to regular binge drinking (more than double the safe amount at a time)

ALCOHOL: How to live longer

Stick to the recommended maximum of 14 units of alcohol per week for women, or 21 for men. Women absorb alcohol more quickly than men because of their higher body fat

Don't save your units for a weekend splurge because binge drinking is especially dangerous. The recommended daily maximum is 2–3 units per day for women and 3–4 for men, and you should have at least a couple of alcohol-free days per week

Don't drink on an empty stomach. Having a glass of milk before you drink, and eating while you're drinking, slows the speed at which alcohol can be absorbed

Don't drink too quickly – allow your liver to keep up. So that's no more than one unit per hour

Alternate alcoholic drinks with soft drinks, and add mixers to your spirits to make them last longer

Don't drink and drive, and don't allow yourself to be driven by anyone who has been drinking

do you have a drink problem?

**It is not only alcoholics who have 'a problem with drink'.
If drink affects your work, your social life, your relationships
or your health then you have a problem.**

Ask yourself the following questions. If you answer 'yes' to any of them,
it's time to change your drinking habits.

☐ Do you regularly get drunk?

☐ Do you slip out to drink at lunchtime, or during the working day?

☐ Do you regularly drink on the way home from work?

☐ Do you find it hard to stop drinking once you have started?

☐ Do you regularly drink alone?

☐ Do you find you need to keep increasing the amount you drink in
order to have the same effect?

☐ Do you forget to keep appointments because you have been
drinking?

☐ Do you have feelings of guilt about the amount you are drinking?

☐ Do you lie about the amount you are drinking?

☐ Do you regularly drink at home, other than with meals?

☐ Have you lost interest in hobbies and sports because they
interfere with your drinking time?

☐ Do you binge drink on more than two days a week?

If you're going to drink...

■ Go slowly – no more than one unit per hour.
  ■ *WHY?* The ethanol in alcoholic drinks is a toxin so, as soon as
  it's absorbed, it's sent straight to the liver to be detoxified. If
  alcohol arrives faster than the liver can handle it, it returns to
  the bloodstream
■ Don't drink on an empty stomach.
  ■ *WHY?* Food slows the absorption of alcohol. Not only will
  this slow down the rate at which the alcohol hits your system,

it will also smooth out blood sugar fluctuations caused by drinking alcohol

■ Alternate alcoholic drinks with non-alcoholic ones.

■ *WHY?* Not only will this slow down your drinking, limiting the amount of alcohol you consume, it will help to rehydrate you. Alcohol is a potent diuretic and will quickly lead to dehydration. And dehydration makes you feel rough – headaches, dizziness… Does any of that sound familiar?

■ Stick to one kind of drink.

■ *WHY?* All alcohol counts towards your 'units' total, but mixing your drinks can increase your chances of having a horrendous hangover the next morning. The saying 'don't mix the grape and the grain' is based on sound science. So, don't mix spirits and wine in an evening

Beneficial booze?

Population studies suggest that people who drink a moderate amount of alcohol – about a glass of wine a day – tend to live longer, and that red wine appears to be the most beneficial tipple. It appears that a natural chemical in wine makes the blood less 'sticky', reducing the risk of dangerous clots.

But new research suggests that alcohol's health benefits may have been exaggerated and, because of the dangers of over indulgence, alcohol certainly shouldn't be promoted as a 'health food'.

The message seems to be, enjoy a glass of wine with your meal if you like, but don't take things to excess.

Watch out for liquid calories

It's easy to forget about the calories you drink. Sugary, fizzy drinks and squashes go down easily, but they pack a hefty calorific punch. Even pure fruit juice is high in sugar so it's best to dilute it with water. This also reduces the damage the acidity can do to your teeth. Alcohol is packed with calories – only fat has more. And since alcohol can make you lose your inhibitions and self-restraint you're more likely to forget about your healthy eating intentions, dealing a double whammy to your waistline! Some people think they're eating fairly healthily, and wonder why they still put on weight. The answer could lie in what they're drinking.

Here's the calorie count for a few favourite drinks:

Beers, lager and cider (half pint)	
Bitter	90 calories
Mild ale	71 calories
Pale ale	91 calories
Brown ale	80 calories
Stout	105 calories
Lager – ordinary strength	85 calories
Dry cider	95 calories
Sweet cider	110 calories
Wine (small 125ml glass)	
Red wine	85 calories
Rose wine	89 calories
White wine (sweet)	118 calories
White wine (medium)	94 calories
White wine (dry)	83 calories
Sparkling white wine	95 calories
Fortified wine (50ml measure)	
Sherry (dry)	58 calories
Sherry (sweet)	68 calories
Vermouth (dry)	52 calories
Vermouth (sweet)	72 calories
Port	79 calories
Spirits (25ml pub measure)	
Vodka, gin, whisky, brandy, rum, etc.	52 calories
Liqueurs (25ml pub measure)	
Tia Maria, Cherry Brandy, Advocaat	66 calories
Cointreau, Drambuie	79 calories
Cream liqueurs	81 calories

And don't forget to add extra calories for the mixers!

Quick fix?

■ *Stick to skimmed milk drinks – ask for a skinny cappuccino or latte.*
■ *Avoid 'coffee whitener' – it's packed with trans fats.*

'Innocent' drinks

And it's not just the booze. Take a look at the milky drinks you enjoy:

1 glass (250ml) chocolate milk	226kcal	9g fat	32g sugar
1 mug (250ml) hot chocolate (whole milk)	225kcal	10g fat	32g sugar

Be careful of the 'designer coffees' in coffee bars. The serving sizes are generally enormous – the largest size latte made with whole milk can tot up 320 kcals and 19g fat, and that's before you add any marshmallows, sugar or flavoured syrups.

But compare a small mug of whole milk with one of skimmed milk:

250ml whole milk	164kcal	9g fat
250ml skimmed milk	82kcal	1.7g fat

Skimmed milk also contains more calcium than whole milk. That's because 'skimming' removes the fat but leaves behind the calcium, which is concentrated in the milk that's left.

What about fizzy drinks and squashes? Some of these contain scary amounts of sugar. A 330ml can of cola contains about 110 calories, and 29g sugar – that's 6 teaspoons!

Squash is also surprisingly high in calories. A large glass, diluted, can give you 85 calories and 20g of sugar. No-added-sugar versions are lower in calories, but do you really want all those dubious artificial sweeteners?

Let's move on to fruit juice – surely that must be healthy? Well, yes, it is a good source of vitamins, and one glass counts towards your '5-portions-per-day'. But fruit juice is a concentrated source of fruit sugars which, although better for you than 'added sugars', still contain just as many calories.

A small 110ml glass (the kind you'd have at breakfast in a hotel) of orange juice contains 58 calories and 14g sugar.

Don't be discouraged from drinking fruit juice, but it's best to dilute it or stick to a glass a day rather than knocking it back like water.

Also, be aware of the difference between 'fruit juice' and 'fruit juice drinks' when you're shopping. Fruit juice drinks are basically squash.

smoking

Stopping smoking – and staying stopped – could be the most important single action you can take to increase the length of your life.

Why it's worth giving up – NOW!

Just look at some of the effects smoking can have on your health:

- Increased risk of lung cancer
- Increased risk of heart disease
- Increased risk of stroke
- Increased risk of emphysema
- Damaged circulation leading to gangrene and possible amputation
- Chronic obstructive pulmonary disease (COPD). (See Your Lungs p. 80)
- Reduced fertility for both men and women, increased risk in pregnancy and risk to baby
- Wheezing, shortness of breath
- Lack of energy
- Poor concentration
- Dull skin, tar-stained fingers, premature wrinkles
- Damaged taste buds and sense of smell, yellow-stained teeth
- Increased risk of fire in the home
- Placing children at higher risk of asthma, cot-death, bronchitis and glue ear. Exposure to smoke is the number one cause of SIDs (cot-death)

And some of the emotional and social consequences of smoking are:

- Turning off potential partners and friends because of smelly mouth, fingers and hair
- A constant nagging sense of guilt that you should give up smoking
- Increased pressure and disapproval from others who don't want to be subjected to second-hand smoke
- Polluting the air for those around you with carcinogens
- Smelly clothes and furniture

Understanding the addiction

Smoking is a complex addiction, not just a bad habit. Scientists believe that nicotine exerts its powerful addictive effects by altering two brain chemicals – dopamine and noradrenaline. Within seven seconds of inhaling nicotine is delivered directly to the brain, where it produces a 'nicotine rush'. Smokers interpret this rush as pleasure, but this is misunderstood. It only seems pleasurable because it is, in reality, simply satisfying the craving created by the previous cigarette. So, over time, the smoker becomes the victim of a vicious cycle of addiction.

SMOKING: Vital statistics

- Every year, around 114,000 smokers in the UK die because of their habit. That's more than 300 each day. It's as if a plane crashed every day and killed all its passengers
- About 50% of all regular cigarette smokers will eventually be killed by their smoking
- 22% of all male deaths and 11% of all female deaths in the UK are due to smoking
- Smoking causes about 30% of all cancer deaths (including around 84% of lung cancer deaths), 17% of all heart disease deaths and at least 80% of deaths from bronchitis and emphysema
- People who smoke and drink alcohol regularly are at greater risk of mouth and throat cancers
- Children whose parents smoke are 1.5 times more likely to develop asthma
- More than 17,000 children under 5 are admitted to hospital every year because of the effects of passive smoking
- More than 80% of smokers start when they're teenagers
- According to national statistics, about 1% of children aged 11 are regular smokers. Between 11 and 15, the figures rise to 7% for boys and 10% for girls
- Tobacco smoke contains over 4,000 chemicals including hydrogen cyanide, ammonia and formaldehyde

Breaking the addiction While breaking the physical addiction to nicotine is hard, for many smokers it is breaking the habit – the psychological addiction – that is the real stumbling block. Over the years you may have lit up a cigarette when you're happy or sad, having to concentrate or are bored, at certain times of the day, whenever you

SMOKING: How to live longer

Giving up smoking can reduce the risk of developing many smoking-related illnesses. And the good news is that within 10–15 years of giving up, an ex-smoker's risk of developing lung cancer is only slightly higher than someone who has never smoked.

are relaxing with a cup of tea or coffee, or after meals. Even when you have made a conscious decision to stop, these smoking associations will take time to disappear.

So when you do decide to quit, remember you are giving up an addiction that may have been with you for years. Don't be too tough on yourself if you find it hard going. Make the most of the support of friends and take advantage of all the help that is on offer. Your doctor's practice may have a specialist clinic or will be able to put you in touch with one.

TOP 10 TIPS FOR QUITTING SMOKING

1 **Prepare mentally.** You will need willpower to break the hold of nicotine, so concentrate on what you will be gaining from the outset.

2 **Know what to expect.** For most people the first few days are a real struggle, but things begin to get better from the third or fourth day. You may feel irritable, restless, anxious, fuzzy-headed and have difficulty sleeping but this is nicotine withdrawal and quickly passes. Keep reminding yourself that they are signs that your body is starting to repair the damage caused by smoking.

3 **Involve friends and family.** Many people find it helpful to have the encouragement of others. Perhaps a friend will quit smoking with you or you may prefer to join a stop-smoking group.

4 **Smoking is often linked to certain times and situations in the day** – with your first cup of tea, talking on the phone, with a drink in the evening. The secret is to break the link between the cigarette and the situation by making changes to your routine. If you always reach for a cigarette with your first cup of coffee in the morning, have a glass of fruit juice or herbal tea instead.

5 **Get active.** When you give up smoking you'll suddenly find yourself with much more energy and the chances are you won't have been doing much exercise. Now is the time to get active. But remember to ask your doctor before starting an exercise programme, especially if you were a heavy smoker. If the doctor gives you the

The average smoker spends £1,750 a year on cigarettes – that's £35,000 over the next 20 years. Just think what you could do with all that money!

Seven out of ten smokers say they want to give up.

go-ahead, join a local gym or exercise class. Try out different kinds of exercise and find one you enjoy. It isn't supposed to be a punishment. If you really don't have time or don't want to go to the gym, there are plenty of everyday activities that will keep you fit and help burn-off calories – try walking, cycling, climbing the stairs, housework and gardening.

6 **Deal with your weight-gain worries.** Yes, it is true that nicotine suppresses your appetite and some people do gain a little weight when they stop smoking. But if you know it's a possibility you can be prepared by eating a healthy diet, cutting down on alcohol and taking more exercise. Remember you will have a great deal more energy when you stop smoking.

7 **If you need something to put into your mouth instead of a cigarette, try sugar-free chewing gum or carrot sticks.** If you need to do something with your hands, find something to fiddle with like a pencil, worry beads or a key ring.

8 **If the urge to smoke creeps up on you, immediately do something to distract yourself** – phone a friend, take a short walk, make a cup of herbal tea or sit down with a good book.

9 **Be kind to yourself in the first few days and weeks and don't try to pack too much into each day.** Make time to relax at the end of the day. It's also a good idea to plan a series of rewards – a massage, a manicure, a walk in the country, an hour in the coffee shop with a friend, a trip to the cinema, an evening in with a video.

10 **Don't give up on giving up.** Research shows that the sooner you stop again, the more likely you are to stop for good. If you lapse, don't beat yourself up about it, but don't let it be an excuse to go straight back to smoking 10 or 20 a day. Use the experience to strengthen your resolve to quit for good. One day you will wake up and realise that you have gone 24 hours without even thinking about a cigarette. Then you'll know you've made it. You are a non-smoker.

mythbuster

The Myth: *Smoking relieves stress.*

The Truth: In reality smokers' lives tend to be more stressful than non-smokers' lives. Think of the smoker and the non-smoker caught in a situation where smoking is not allowed. Which one is the more likely to be distracted, fidgety and longing to get outside to light up? Stop smoking and you remove a cause of stress.

Cut the cravings

Nicotine replacement therapy (NRT) and Zyban are available to help reduce the physical cravings associated with nicotine withdrawal. You can buy most NRT products at local chemists and supermarkets or get them on prescription. Zyban is only available on prescription from a doctor.

NRT provides the body with nicotine without the dangerous tar, carbon monoxide and the other poisonous chemicals in tobacco smoke. It's designed to ease the withdrawal while you become a non-smoker. Once the cravings go, you phase out the NRT.

NRT is available in a number of forms – skin patches, chewing gum, nasal spray, inhalators and lozenges. You can get advice on which may suit you best from a specialist NHS advisor. Smokers report that NRT in the form of gum is more effective than patches.

Zyban, like all drugs, has possible side effects. It works by suppressing the part of the brain that gives you a nicotine buzz when you smoke. It helps to reduce cravings and withdrawal symptoms.

Stubbing it out

The good news Give up smoking and your body will start feeling the benefits just minutes after you've taken your last puff.

Did you know that in:

- **20 minutes** — Blood pressure and pulse rate return to normal
- **1 hour** — Circulation starts to improve
- **20 hours** — Carbon monoxide is removed from your body. Oxygen levels rise and you have more energy
- **24 hours** — No nicotine left in the body. Taste and smell greatly improved
- **72 hours** — Breathing becomes easier
- **2–12 weeks** — Circulation throughout the body improves, and your skin looks better
- **3–9 months** — Lung function is increased by up to 10%
- **1 year** — Risk of a heart attack falls to half that of a smoker
- **10 years** — Risk of lung cancer falls to half that of a smoker
- **15 years** — Risk of heart attack falls to that of a non-smoker

drugs

It's well known that drug overdoses can kill, and that long-term drug abuse can wreck your body and your life. It's impossible to tease out just how many deaths can be blamed on drugs, since their use pervades every part of an addict's life. Drug users often smoke and drink excessively, or indulge in unsafe sex, and may even turn to crime to finance their habit. But it is possible to say that drug abuse can cause:

- Damage to the body's organs, sometimes with fatal results
- Depression and suicide
- Poisoning due to mixing drugs
- Poisoning due to use of contaminated drugs
- Death due to involvement in a criminal lifestyle
- Deaths due to motor accidents – drug-driving
- Hepatitis B and C from shared needles
- HIV/AIDS from shared needles
- Destruction of relationships with family and friends
- Loss of job
- Homelessness

And even occasional use can be hazardous, not least because it can set you on the slippery slope towards addiction.

Addiction is characterised by:

- Higher tolerance: needing more and more of the drug to get the same effect
- Withdrawal symptoms that disappear when more of the drug is taken

It's not just illegal drugs that are a problem – people can also be addicted to:

- Prescription medicines (such as tranquillisers, sleeping tablets or painkillers)
- Over-the-counter medicines (such as cough mixtures, painkillers or herbal remedies)

DRUGS: How to live longer

If you have a problem, admit and accept that it exists

Seek help – start with your GP, who can refer you to a specialist

If you don't feel you can talk to your GP, try your local drug dependence unit (DDU), or community drug project (CDP)

Don't just try to go cold turkey. It probably won't work and could be dangerous

Remember that you'll have to cope with both the physical (chemical) addiction to the drug, and also the psychological addiction

Stick at it. It won't be easy, and recovery can be a long process

Contact the National Drugs Helpline (see Appendix 1) or one of the many help groups. Being able to talk to someone who understands, and also with former addicts who've 'been there', can make the difference between failure and success

DRUGS: Vital statistics

- It is estimated that almost 11 million adults in England and Wales have used illicit drugs (ever) and approximately 3.5 million have used them in the past year
- Just under 4 million adults have used Class A drugs in their lifetime, with just over 1 million having used them in the past year
- The most recent Home Office British Crime Survey found that 35% of adults had used one or more illicit drugs in their lifetime
- 11.3% had used one or more illicit drugs in the past year
- 7% had used one or more illicit drugs in the last month
- Cannabis was the drug most likely to be used, followed by cocaine, then ecstasy and amphetamines

stress

You need a certain amount of pressure to function effectively – it heightens your senses and speeds up your reactions. But when stress pushes you beyond your own personal limits, even things that are normally a piece of cake become mountainous obstacles.

It's this chronic, long-term stress that so many of us are under today that can play havoc with our health. It's not just an urban myth that stressed-out executives are more likely to drop dead of a heart attack. Stress really can take years off your life.

Chronic stress:
- Raises your blood pressure
- Increases your risk of heart disease and stroke
- Suppresses your immune system so that you're more vulnerable to every bug and germ that comes your way
- Hinders wound healing
- Depletes the levels of vitamins and other nutrients in your body
- Can lead to migraines
- Exacerbates hayfever
- Contributes to arthritis
- Increases cancer risk
- Reduces fertility
- Can cause stomach ulcers

Dr Una says...

What happens when you're stressed? Chronic stress occurs when your body reacts to long-term mental pressures as though they were immediate physical dangers by preparing itself for action; this is commonly described as 'fight or flee'. The hypothalamus in the brain reacts by automatically sending messages to the adrenal glands. These glands release stress hormones – adrenaline and noradrenaline – which circulate around the body, gearing up your cells so they are ready for action.

The stress hormones cause the body to:
- Release fats and sugar into the blood to provide extra energy for the muscles

- Speed up breathing so that you can take in more oxygen
- Thicken the blood so that it will clot easily if you're injured
- Speed up the heart rate, raising blood pressure, to supply blood to the muscles
- Divert blood from the digestive system to the muscles
- Tense the muscles
- Speed up your reaction time
- Increase your aggressive feelings

Stay friends with your partner

Bickering with your partner can hamper the body's natural healing processes. Studies have shown that after an argument with their partner or spouse, people heal slower from injuries.

This was all very well when our ancestors faced a hungry sabre-toothed tiger, or when a modern-day mother needs superhuman reactions and strength to pull her child out of the way of a car. But the body reacts in the same way to things like traffic jams, call-centre queues and money worries, and being in a constant state of stress isn't good for you. It places unnecessary strain on the heart, diverts energy from the digestive system causing stomach upsets, and depletes your body of several important vitamins.

It's important to learn to differentiate between temporary stress that disappears as soon as a situation is resolved, and long-term continuous stress. Most people can cope with short periods of stress, but chronic stress can be psychologically and emotionally damaging.

Stress and the immune response Several scientific studies have shown that chronic stress suppresses the immune system, making you more vulnerable to infection, and also hampering your body's defences against cancer. Scientists measured the levels of stress hormones in people caring for relatives with Alzheimer's. The worry the carers experienced appeared to increase their stress levels and suppress their immune systems, something that may contribute to the development of new diseases, or hasten the progression of existing illnesses.

WHAT CAUSES STRESS?

A wide range of things, or even just the fear of them happening, can cause stress:

- Illness or injury
- Pressure at work, at school or at college
- Financial worries
- Conflicts in the family
- Divorce
- Bereavement
- Unemployment
- Moving house
- Changing jobs

Often there is no principal trigger for developing stress. It may arise from a series of minor problems over a period of time.

Warning signs These are just some of the warning signs that your stress levels may be higher than is good for your health:

- Difficulty concentrating
- Memory lapses
- Feeling out of control
- Panic attacks
- Constant anxiety
- Depression
- Lack of confidence
- Crying
- Lack of self-esteem
- Smoking more than usual
- Eating more or less than usual
- Difficulty in sleeping
- Headaches or dizzy spells
- Losing your temper over trivial things
- Tension in your shoulders and neck

STRESS: Vital statistics

- People in the UK spend an average of 26 hours per week feeling stressed, with women suffering more than men, according to a 2006 major survey by a healthcare company
- The main cause of stress is family issues (45% of people, especially between the ages of 30–50)
- Money was the next biggest stress factor, reported by 39% of people
- A smaller proportion – 37% of the total population (40% of women) – felt anxious about their health and diet
- 25% reported being stressed about their job

are you stressed?

1 How would you assess your ability to deal with stress?
[0] I can manage my stress levels
[1] I can usually manage my stress levels
[2] I feel unable to cope with even small amounts of stress

2 Are there times when you feel your life is out of control?
[0] Never
[1] Occasionally
[2] Regularly

3 Do you find it hard to concentrate on simple tasks?
[0] Never
[1] Occasionally
[2] Regularly

4 Do you find yourself dissolving into tears?
[0] Never
[1] Occasionally
[2] Regularly

5 Do you suffer from panic attacks?
[0] Never
[1] Rarely
[2] At least once a week

6 Do you lose your temper over trivial things?
[0] Never
[1] Occasionally
[2] Often

7 Do you regularly have difficulty sleeping?
[0] No
[1] Yes

8 Do you suffer from headaches and tense neck and shoulder muscles?
[0] Never
[1] Occasionally
[2] Often

Now add up your score:
0–3: You seem to have got stress licked. We all face stress in our lives but your coping strategies are working for you. Keep up the good work.

4–7: You're getting there. Although you are occasionally stressed you are mostly able to keep it in check.

8–12: You're obviously feeling the effects of stress. Take a look at your life and try to find ways of reducing stress at home and at work.

13–15: Your stress levels are almost certainly affecting your health. It's time to make some changes. If your own efforts don't help, you need to seek professional advice.

Quick Relaxation Fixes!

- *Find a quiet place. Breathe in deeply through your nose, hold your breath for a moment then breathe out loudly through your mouth. Repeat five times.*

- *Shrug your shoulders up towards your ears, then relax them downwards. Repeat five times.*

- *Try 'palming'. If you work in front of a computer, sit back for a moment and cup your hands over your eyes and relax for a few seconds.*

- *Take a break. Make yourself a cup of tea – try chamomile or rooibosch – and take time to relax while you drink it.*

Managing Stress

Try to identify the cause of your stress. Although sometimes you may not be able to change or avoid stressful situations, on other occasions just making simple changes to your lifestyle will reduce your stress. The key to managing stress is to find a method or a range of methods that work for you.

Time and again, studies show that it's not 'stress' itself that puts you at risk of early death but the coping strategies you use to deal with it. People with good coping skills find it easier to brush off stress, while those who resort to bad coping skills suffer the health consequences.

STRESS: How to live longer

Learn to delegate or share responsibilities at work and at home

Avoid confrontation when you can

Learn to be more assertive (not aggressive!)

Share your problems and fears with family and friends

Realise that there are things you can't do anything about – then try to stop worrying about them

Eat a healthy diet and take regular exercise

Learn to organise your time so that you can prioritise the tasks you need to achieve each day. Time management is a key step in helping you to keep tabs on your stress

Learn to say 'No' – and mean it

Get enough sleep (see tips on p. 177)

Good coping skills

- Maintaining a good sense of humour
- Taking 'time out' (for example, having interests outside your work)
- Taking exercise
- Good time management and prioritising
- Being able to have a good moan
- Being able to talk to your friends and colleagues
- Planning your day
- Using relaxation techniques, such as breathing exercises
- Having a positive mental attitude
- Maintaining your confidence
- Remaining flexible about your options
- Taking food and drink breaks
- Being able to ask for help
- Being able to just say 'NO'!
- Guilt-free delegation
- Having a visual distraction, such as a nice view from your window, or a photo of your family or holiday to look at

Bad coping skills

- Alcohol (in excess)
- Swearing (in excess)
- Smoking
- Not taking time out after a heated disagreement or stressful encounter
- Poor communication
- Self-blame after a stressful encounter – thinking why it happened
- Failing to empathise with the other person's point of view – that is, always blaming them
- Taking it out on others – your family, friends or your pet
- Letting things build up
- Overworking, and taking work home
- Indiscretion – for example, having an affair, fraud, theft, etc.
- Doing everything yourself
- Denying that you have a problem

Relaxation

Relaxation is one of the most effective weapons against stress. Not only does it help you to repair the damage of a 'stress overload' it helps to protect you against stress and gives you a feeling of 'being in control'.

Often a simple change of activity will reduce your feelings of stress. But total relaxation is more than just putting your feet up. You need to switch off and wind down.

Try some of these relaxation strategies:

Deep breathing

Sit or stand in a quiet room. Take ten deep, slow breaths, in through the nose and out through the mouth.

Relax your muscles

When you are stressed you may tense your muscles, particularly in the neck, jaw and shoulders. Consciously relax your muscles.

Visualisation

Close your eyes and bring to mind a place that holds happy memories for you. Visualise it and watch the scene unfold as you hear the sounds and smell the scents.

Yoga or meditation

Find a yoga class or learn meditation techniques.

Stress and nutrition

Stress also depletes your body's nutrient levels so it's particularly important to eat healthily when you're stressed, to top up those vital reserves.

Pay special attention to the B vitamins, vitamin C, and antioxidants – these are responsible for energy release in our bodies, as well as wound healing and supporting our immune systems. You can see how being deficient could leave you below par.

Eat plenty of colourful fruit and vegetables, wholegrains, nuts and seeds to replace the nutrients sapped by stress. Don't turn to heavy drinking or smoking as a 'prop' when you're stressed. As well as harming your body directly, they also deplete your nutrient levels even further.

When to see a doctor

If stress is causing physical symptoms, distress or making it difficult for you to function normally, it's time to see a doctor. Extreme or prolonged stress can lead to medical problems that may need treatment.

CHAPTER 5

YOU AND YOUR VITAL ORGANS

your heart

Heart disease is a vague and woolly term that covers several conditions, but the main ones we're concerned about here are those you can do something about by changing your lifestyle.

Coronary Artery Disease This occurs when the blood vessels supplying the heart – the coronary arteries – become furred up. (See p. 75 for more information on clogged arteries.) This can lead to angina, a heavy, uncomfortable feeling in the chest, which usually occurs when you exert yourself or are upset. Angina is caused by not enough blood reaching the heart via the clogged arteries.

Clogged arteries can also lead to a heart attack (or 'myocardial infarction'), which occurs when one of the coronary arteries is blocked by a blood clot or a cholesterol plaque. Part of the heart muscle is then starved of oxygenated blood and is damaged or dies.

> *Your heart weighs about 300g, and pumps nearly 8,000 litres of blood a day.*

Coronary Heart Disease (CHD) This is an umbrella term covering coronary artery disease, angina and heart attacks. It's what is usually meant by 'heart disease'.

Heart failure This doesn't mean that the heart has completely stopped working! Heart failure means that the heart has trouble working effectively and can't pump enough blood around the body. The result is breathlessness at night or when walking, tiredness and a build-up of fluid in the body, particularly in the ankles or feet. Heart failure may be caused by damage to the heart from a heart attack. It can also be caused by high blood pressure, a heart rate that is too fast or too slow, problems with the heart valves or with the heart muscle itself.

HEART DISEASE: Vital statistics

- Coronary heart disease is the number one cause of premature death in the UK, accounting for 22% of premature deaths in men and 12% in women. Nearly all of these are due to heart attacks
- Coronary heart disease accounts for 1 in 5 adult deaths – that's around 114,000 per year in the UK

- Every year, around 260,000 people in the UK suffer heart attacks
- In the last 10 years, the death rate from coronary heart disease among the over-65s has fallen by 40%. But the number of people actually suffering from heart problems is increasing. And these people are at a higher risk of dying before their time.
  - *2 million people suffer from angina*
  - *1.3 million have had a heart attack*
  - *Up to 800,000 are suffering from heart failure*
- Coronary heart disease costs the UK Health Service £350,000 million each year

Because of the protective effect of the female hormone oestrogen, younger women are less likely to develop clogged arteries (atherosclerosis). But after the menopause, when a woman's body produces less oestrogen, her heart disease risk rises until it is approximately the same as a man's.

mythbuster

The Myth: *Heart disease is something only middle-aged, stressed-out male executives suffer from.*

The Truth: Heart disease is the number one killer of women. And while heart disease rates among men are falling, they are rising for women.

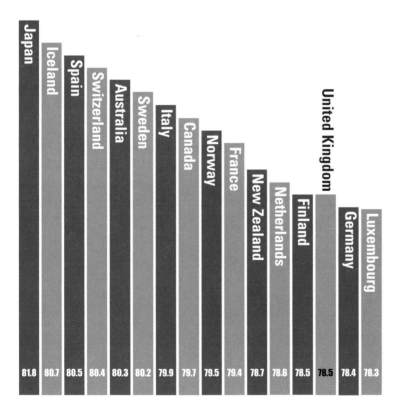

Japan	Iceland	Spain	Switzerland	Australia	Sweden	Italy	Canada	Norway	France	New Zealand	Netherlands	Finland	United Kingdom	Germany	Luxembourg
81.8	80.7	80.5	80.4	80.3	80.2	79.9	79.7	79.5	79.4	78.7	78.6	78.5	78.5	78.4	78.3

Average life expectancy in years

Copyright OECD HEALTH DATA 2005, October 05

what's your risk of heart attack?

This quiz is designed to get you thinking about the things that affect your heart disease risk. If any of the answers to your questions worry you, or make you think you may be at risk, talk to your doctor. Heart disease kills and it's not worth taking any chances if there's something you could be doing to protect yourself.

1 Heart disease risk increases with age. How old are you?

[0]   Under 45

[3]   46–59

[8]   60–70

[10] 70+

2 Men, and women after the menopause, have a higher heart disease risk. Are you…?

[3]   Male

[0]   Female – before menopause

[3]   Female – after menopause

3 Did your father develop heart disease before the age of 55, or your mother before 65?

[7]   Yes, both mother and father

[6]   Yes, mother or father

[0]   No

4 What is your cholesterol level?

[0]   Under 5 mmol/litre

[4]   5–5.5 mmol/litre

[6]   5.6–6.5 mmol/litre

[9]   Over 6.5 mmol/litre

[9]   I don't know my cholesterol level

5 How does your doctor describe your blood pressure?

[0]   Low or normal

[3]   Borderline high

[5]   High

[8]   Very high

[8]   Don't know my blood pressure

6 Do you smoke?

[14]   Yes

[0]   No – never smoked, or gave up more than 15 years ago

[6]   No – gave up in the last year

[4]   No – gave up 1–15 years ago

7 What is your body mass index? (See p. 37 to work it out.)

[0]   Below 25

[1]   25–29

[3]   30–35

[5]   36+

8 'Apple-shaped' people who store fat around their bellies have a higher heart risk than 'pear-shaped' people who lay down fat on their bottom and thighs. What is your waist-to-hip measurement ratio? (See p. 39 to work this out.)

[0]   Ratio under 0.85 for women (under 0.9 for men)

[4]   Ratio over 0.85 for women (under 0.9 for men)

9 Do you suffer from diabetes?

[15]   Yes

[0]   No

10 How many portions of fruit and vegetables do you eat in a day?

[3]   0–3

[1]   4–6

[0]   More than 6

11 Processed foods, such as ready meals, are often high in salt, fat and sugar, all things that can contribute to heart disease risk factors. How often do you eat processed foods?

[2] Every day

[1] More than 3 times a week

[0] Less than twice a week

12 How often do you eat fast foods like burgers, chips and kebabs?

[3] Every day

[1] 3–6 days a week

[0] Less than twice a week

13 How often do you achieve 30 minutes of moderate exercise in a week (for example, brisk walking)?

[0] Every day

[2] 4–6 times a week or less

[4] 2–3 times a week

[7] Rarely or never

14 How many units of alcohol do you drink each day? (1 unit = a small glass of wine, a measure of spirits or a half-pint of beer)

[1] I'm teetotal

[0] Average of 2 or fewer (3 for men) units per day

[3] Average of 3–4 (4–6 for men) units per day

[6] Average of 5 or more (7 or more for men) units per day

Now add up your score:
Under 25: Low risk.

36–45: Low to moderate risk.

46–55: Moderate to high risk.

Over 55: High risk.

You may have found that not knowing your blood pressure or cholesterol skewed your result to give you a higher 'risk score' than you expected. Go to your doctor and get them checked – then you'll know your risk and can start to take the necessary steps to protect your heart.

HEART DISEASE: How to live longer

There's a lot you can do to reduce your risk of heart attack and other heart problems.

■ Eat a heart-healthy diet

Plenty of fruit and vegetables, and nuts and seeds, for antioxidants.

Cut down your total fat intake, and replace saturated and trans fats with unsaturated fats.

Eat oily fish at least twice a week, but no more than twice if you're pregnant or planning a baby.

Cut down your salt intake – that means no more than 6g salt (2.4g sodium) per day.

Eat garlic – it can help lower your levels of 'bad' LDL cholesterol.

■ Watch your weight – it's risky to be overweight, or underweight.

■ Do aerobic or cardiovascular exercise that works the heart and lungs – enough to make you feel warm and out of breath. If you're unfit, ease in gradually – it needn't be especially strenuous. A large-scale study found that women who walked briskly for at least three hours a week were 30% less likely to develop heart disease.

■ Give up smoking, and avoid smoky places.

■ Don't drink alcohol excessively – a drink or two in an evening is fine, but don't overdo it.

■ Have your blood pressure and cholesterol levels checked regularly.

blood pressure

High blood pressure (hypertension) can take years off your life. It:

BLOOD PRESSURE: How to live longer

TURN BACK YOUR BODY CLOCK

The good news is that there's a lot you can do to keep your blood pressure below the danger line, and even to lower it if it's too high.

Have your blood pressure measured

Don't eat too much salt

Don't drink more than the recommended amount

Don't smoke

Take a sensible amount of exercise

Relax, and reduce the stress in your life

Watch your weight

Eat 'good' mono- and poly-unsaturated fats to keep your heart healthy. (See Fats p. 40–44 for more information)

Eat vegetables and vegetable protein rather than animal protein. Studies suggest that a vegetarian diet helps to lower blood pressure

- Increases your risk of heart attacks
- Increases your risk of strokes
- Can lead to the heart becoming enlarged and inefficient
- Can lead to kidney problems
- Can lead to eye problems

A lot of your blood pressure is genetically determined and blood pressure increases gradually and naturally as you grow older – but your lifestyle plays an important part, too.

HIGH BLOOD PRESSURE: Vital statistics

- 1 in 4 adults in the UK suffers from high blood pressure
- One-third of these don't even know it. The only way to find out is to have your blood pressure measured
- High blood pressure makes you three times more likely to develop heart disease or have a stroke, and twice as likely to die from these diseases than if you had normal blood pressure

What do the numbers mean?

When your blood pressure is measured, you'll be told two numbers. The first, higher, number is called the 'systolic blood pressure', and this is recorded when the pulse rate is first heard and represents the highest amount of pressure in the arteries. The lower number is the 'diastolic blood pressure' and represents the lowest amount of pressure in the arteries at rest. You're aiming for 130/85 (and even lower if you're diabetic, as you are more likely to have high blood pressure, which is riskier for diabetics). Optimal blood pressure is 120/80 or less.

If you can maintain your blood pressure below 130/85 you almost certainly won't have a heart attack or a stroke. If you've already got high blood pressure, reducing it by 5 mmHg can reduce the risk of having a heart attack by about 16%. If changing your lifestyle fails to lower your blood pressure enough, your doctor may have to prescribe medication.

clogged arteries

Furring-up of the arteries (atherosclerosis) doesn't happen overnight – it sneaks up on you gradually. Often there are no symptoms at all until – wham! – you have a heart attack or stroke.

Gradually, over the years, the artery walls can take up cholesterol, becoming thickened and hard and form so-called 'arterial plaques'. This narrows the arteries, restricting the flow of blood.

The plaques are delicate and, if they rupture, blood clots can form which block the artery and stop the blood flow. Sometimes the clot sits where it is, or it can break away and travel around the blood system until it lodges somewhere else.

These blood clots cause big problems:
- Clots in the brain = strokes
- Clots in the coronary arteries = heart attack

There are various risk factors:
- Age. Incidence is more frequent after 45 years old
- Family history
- Being male
- Being overweight or obese
- Not exercising enough
- Diabetes
- Smoking
- Excessive alcohol consumption

CLOGGED ARTERIES: How to live longer

TURN BACK YOUR BODY CLOCK

Maintain a healthy weight

Exercise regularly

Eat a heart-healthy diet
- *Low fat (though with enough 'good' mono- and poly-unsaturated fats)*
- *High fibre*
- *Plenty of fruit and vegetables – the antioxidants they contain help protect the arteries and reduce the risk of ruptures and clots*

Quit smoking

Drink sensibly – no more than 14 units per week for women or 21 for men, and no bingeing!

Have your cholesterol level checked regularly

cholesterol

Cholesterol is bad for you, right? Well, yes and no. Too much cholesterol can clog your arteries, increasing your risk of heart disease and stroke. But cholesterol is also vital for your body's normal functioning – it forms part of our cell membranes and nerves, and it's needed to make hormones.

The Myth: *All cholesterol is 'bad' and you should cut it out of your diet.*

The Truth: Cholesterol is so vital to your body that your body makes it itself! For years the advice was to avoid foods that were high in cholesterol, such as eggs and prawns. But the British Heart Foundation now says it's fine to have four eggs a week – even if you suffer from iffy cholesterol levels – as long as you eat an overall healthy diet. The amount of cholesterol your body makes itself is affected by the foods you eat. So the best way to avoid clogged arteries is to avoid the foods that stimulate your body to churn out too much cholesterol of its own.

Good and bad cholesterol To muddy the water further there are good and bad kinds of cholesterol:

- HDL cholesterol is the 'good' kind because it shuttles cholesterol to the liver where it can be broken down. HDL helps protect you from heart disease
- LDL cholesterol is the 'bad' kind. It hangs around in the blood circulation where it can be taken up by the artery walls, leading to thickening known as atherosclerosis or 'furring up' of the arteries. Clogged arteries restrict the blood flow, contributing to heart problems such as angina and heart attacks

CHOLESTEROL: Vital statistics

- Only about 20% of your blood cholesterol comes directly from cholesterol in your food – the other 80% is made by your body
- Eating healthily can reduce your cholesterol levels by 5–10%
- Men tend to have higher cholesterol levels than women
- 1 in 500 people suffer from an inherited condition called familial hyperlipidaemia, which makes the body produce too much cholesterol

What to aim for

- Total cholesterol level under 5 mmol/l
- LDL level under 3 mmol/l
- HDL level above 1 mmol/l
- Triglyceride level under 2 mmol/l.

CHOLESTEROL: How to live longer

The good news is that you can do a lot to reduce your cholesterol levels. However, sometimes even this fails to reduce them to safe levels, and your doctor will need to prescribe cholesterol-lowering drugs.

You should also:

■ Cut down on your total fat intake, by limiting fatty or fried foods, crisps, pastry and biscuits

■ Cut down your intake of saturated and trans fats in particular – they increase your level of 'bad' LDL cholesterol

■ Mono-unsaturated fats lower your 'bad' cholesterol levels. So, eat vegetable oils such as olive oil.

■ Poly-unsaturated fats also lower your 'bad' cholesterol levels. So, eat oily fish such as salmon, mackerel, sardines and fresh tuna for poly-unsaturated Omega-3s. Eat nuts and seeds for poly-unsaturated Omega-6s.

■ Replace your usual spread with one enriched with plant sterols or plant stanols. Check the packaging. These natural compounds have been scientifically proven to help lower cholesterol levels

■ Eat garlic. It can help reduce blood lipids (fats) and total blood cholesterol, but without lowering levels of 'good' HDL cholesterol

■ Maintain a healthy weight. If you're overweight, every 10% of your bodyweight that you lose can cut your cholesterol by 10% and increase your 'good' HDL cholesterol by 8%

■ Take plenty of exercise. Half an hour of exercise, five times a week, can increase HDL cholesterol

■ Eat plenty of fruit and vegetables to provide antioxidants and protect your arteries

■ Eat cholesterol-lowering superfoods, such as oats

■ Have your cholesterol level checked regularly

■ If you do have high cholesterol levels, there are cholesterol-lowering drugs called statins available without a prescription from your pharmacist. Ask your pharmacist or doctor if they would be beneficial for you. Your doctor may also prescribe you a statin if you are at risk of heart disease

shake the salt habit

Too much salt can raise your blood pressure, increasing your risk of heart disease and stroke, as well as making you more vulnerable to stomach cancer. Thanks to better public awareness, salt intakes are falling, but the average intake in the UK is still way too high.

How much is too much?

You shouldn't eat more than 6g of salt per day (less for children). That's just over 1 teaspoon. You may think you don't eat a lot of salt, particularly if you don't sprinkle much or any in your cooking or on your plate when you're eating. But 75% of the salt in our diets comes from processed foods.

Salt or sodium?

It's actually the sodium in salt that's bad for you because it causes your body to retain too much water in the blood vessels, which increases your blood pressure with all the heart risks that entails. So many food labels list sodium as well as or instead of salt – which can make things confusing. Salt is made up of sodium plus chlorine, so however much sodium a food contains in grams, it will contain more grams of salt. Here's how to figure it out. The amount of salt is the amount of sodium multiplied by 2.5. So a food that contains 1.5g of sodium per portion has 1.5 x 2.5 = 3.75g of salt per portion. And that's well on the way towards your 6g daily salt maximum. Another way of looking at it is to remember you shouldn't have more than 2.4g sodium per day.

The Myth: *My food won't taste of anything if I don't add salt.*

The Truth: Your food will taste of food, not salt! Although you may miss the salty taste at first, if you cut down gradually you won't miss it so much. Soon, eating foods the way you used to will taste horribly salty!

Salt check

Cut down on these salty foods: Anchovies, bacon, cheese, crisps and pretzels, gravy granules, olives, pickles, salted and dry roasted nuts, sausages, smoked meat and fish, soy sauce, stock cubes, yeast extract (for example, Marmite and Vegemite).

You'll also find salt 'hidden' in foods such as: Bread, crackers, breakfast cereals, biscuits (even sweet ones), tinned spaghetti, stir-in sauces, ready meals, baked beans, table sauces such as tomato ketchup, tinned vegetables and beans, soups.

SALT: How to live longer

- Make as much of your food as possible – that way you control the salt content.

- Read the labels – try to avoid foods with 1.25g salt or more per 100g (0.5g sodium or more per 100g). That's a lot of salt.

- Aim for foods with 0.25g salt or less per 100g (0.1g sodium or less per 100g). This is only a little salt (for a processed food).

- Cut down on cured foods such as bacon and foods packed in brine, such as olives.

- Soy sauce is extremely salty. Treat it as you would salt.

- Look at the amount of salt you're adding while cooking. Don't just tip it into your hand and straight into the saucepan. Instead get a small salt spoon and gradually decrease the amount you are adding over a few weeks. Research has shown that if salt is decreased slowly no one will notice.

- Instead of salt, use herbs and spices to season your cooking.

- Instead of buying ready-made pasta sauces, make your own using tomatoes, mushrooms, onions, tomato juice, fresh herbs and ground black pepper. You can do it in the time it takes the pasta to cook.

- Taste food before you add salt and then only add a little at a time if you need it.

- Make marinades and spicy rubs to add flavour to meat, poultry and fish, rather than seasoning with salt.

- Take the salt off the dining table. If you have to go and get it, you might decide not to bother.

- Steam vegetables without salt, and then add just a little during the last two minutes of cooking time.

- If you're making a dish from a recipe use half the amount of salt stated and adjust the seasoning if necessary just before you are ready to serve.

Quick and healthy pasta sauce recipe

1 small can chopped tomatoes
1 small onion, peeled and chopped
6 mushrooms, wiped and thinly sliced
1 clove garlic
½ tsp olive oil
½ tsp sugar
Freshly ground black pepper

Put the oil into a non-stick pan and cook the onion and garlic until softened. Add the mushrooms and cook for one minute, then add the remaining ingredients. Simmer gently for 8–10 minutes. Add drained, cooked pasta and stir. Cook for a couple of minutes to reheat the pasta and serve.

your lungs

Lung problems – excluding lung cancer – are the third biggest killer in the UK after cardiovascular disease and cancer. They are also the most common illnesses responsible for emergency admissions to hospital.

COPD: How to live longer

If you smoke, quit! If you already suffer from it, quitting the deadly weed will slow the disease's progression

Try to avoid pollution, dust and fumes. Wear a good-quality mask if you have to work with toxic substances and fumes

If you suffer from symptoms of phlegm, coughing and breathlessness see your doctor. COPD can be diagnosed by a simple test (called spirometry) in your GP's surgery. A spirometer is a hand-held device that measures the amount of air you can breathe out. The two most important readings in spirometry are the amount you can breathe out in one breath and the amount you can breathe out in one second. All you have to do is take a deep breath in, then forcibly exhale into the spirometer's mouthpiece

Take aerobic exercise to help keep your lungs healthy

Chronic obstructive pulmonary disease (COPD)

The main respiratory disease in the UK is COPD. This umbrella term covers a group of severe problems affecting different parts of the respiratory system – emphysema, chronic bronchitis and small airways disease.

COPD occurs when damage and narrowing in the respiratory system causes coughing and difficulty in breathing. It's scary, it can kill and once the damage is done it's irreversible. It is the only major cause of death in the UK that is increasing, and while rates appear to have levelled off in men they are increasing in women.

Causes of COPD:

- Smoking and passive smoking – the main cause
- Dust, fumes and other pollutants
- And, rarely, a genetic condition

In its early stages, many sufferers blame their symptoms on 'smoker's cough' and by the time they're actually diagnosed with COPD a lot of damage has occurred. One of the worst things about COPD is suffering a sudden 'flare-up' or 'lung attack', where you feel that you are suffocating or drowning. Flare-ups generally mean a hospital stay and almost half of patients are either back in hospital – or dead – within three months. At best, flare-ups can seriously weaken your health.

COPD: Vital statistics

- COPD and related conditions kill around 27,000 people every year in the UK
- 10% of the UK population show signs of COPD
- It's estimated that 3 million suffer from COPD in the UK but only 25% of these have actually been diagnosed
- 1 in 8 hospital admissions are caused by COPD
- As many as 50% of smokers will develop COPD

ASTHMA

Asthma causes the airways to become sensitive and inflamed. When a person with asthma comes into contact with an asthma trigger, the airway linings swell, making it hard to breathe. People often think of asthma as a childhood disease, but 40% of sufferers are diagnosed after their eighteenth birthday and 25% aren't diagnosed until after they're 35.

ASTHMA: Vital statistics

- 5.2 million people in the UK are currently receiving treatment for asthma: 1.1 million children (1 in 10) and 4.1 million adults (1 in 12)
- On average, 1,400 people die from asthma each year in the UK – almost four people per day, or one person every seven hours
- There are over 69,000 annual hospital admissions for asthma in the UK. That's around 190 per day
- Half of the UK's 2.6 million asthma sufferers have severe symptoms that have a huge impact on their daily lives, with attacks so severe they cannot speak and may have to be admitted to hospital

ASTHMA: How to live longer

'Occupational asthma' can develop due to exposure to chemicals such as latex, sawdust, flour and fumes. If you work in an industry where you breathe in potential irritants (for example, you're a hairdresser, baker or paint sprayer), see your doctor as soon as you notice any asthma symptoms. Your chances of controlling your condition are better the earlier you catch it.

A lot of research is being conducted into what causes adult-onset asthma, including heavy bodyweight. Obesity appears to be associated with an increased incidence of asthma

*Things that could decrease your risk:
Antioxidants and Omega-3 fatty acids. Due to their anti-inflammatory effect, these food components could help reduce your risk of asthma and manage it if you're a sufferer. Find them in fruit, vegetables and oily fish*

The fitter you are, the better your lung function, and exercise also appears to reduce your risk of asthma

your liver

If your liver shut down completely you would be dead within 24 hours. It is the workhorse of your body's organs. It is the body's largest organ, about the size and shape of a rugby ball, and it's powerful. But it has an enormous amount of work to deal with and sometimes it can't cope.

Dr Una says...

It's impossible to give a quick answer to the question 'what does the liver do?' It is the body's main processing plant – a chemical factory responsible for over 500 chemical reactions and processes in the body, including:

- Removing toxins (including alcohol) and waste products from the blood
- Producing haemoglobin, the substance that makes blood red and carries oxygen around the body
- Making clotting factors to stop bleeding when you're injured
- Removing old red-blood cells from the circulation and recycling them
- Helping to regulate blood sugar levels
- Building up protein from amino acids in our digested food
- Making the cholesterol that we need
- Producing bile, which is stored in the gallbladder and helps break down fat in the digestive system. Making bile also requires cholesterol so the liver grabs excess cholesterol from your bloodstream – which has to be a good thing
- Resisting infections by producing immune factors and removing bacteria from the bloodstream

The liver is incredibly hardwearing. It can continue to operate when 75% of the liver cells are out of action and constantly grows new liver cells. If some of the liver were removed, it would grow back to its normal size within a few weeks.

The liver also acts as a warehouse:
- It stores energy, by converting glucose to glycogen. The glycogen can then later be converted back into glucose which is released into the bloodstream when your blood sugar levels fall too low and you need energy
- It stores iron and also the fat-soluble vitamins, including vitamins A, D, E and K

What can go wrong? These are the main liver problems in the UK:

- Fatty liver – this can be the first stage of alcoholic liver damage. It's a 'side-effect' of the liver having to break down so much alcohol. Fatty liver can also be linked with obesity and diabetes
- Hepatitis – an inflamed liver – can be caused by:
  - *Too much alcohol*
  - *Viruses (hepatitis A, B and C)*
  - *Drug use*
  - *Exposure to some chemical pollutants and toxins*
- Cirrhosis of the liver – where the damage progresses so that areas of the liver become scarred and are destroyed
- Cancer

Most cases of liver disease are caused by long-term over-indulgence in alcohol. If the problem is nipped in the bud, the liver can regenerate, but if an inflamed liver progresses to cirrhosis, liver scarring and destruction is the result. This is irreversible. Sometimes so much of the liver is destroyed that it simply can't cope with its workload and stops working completely. This is liver failure, and a liver transplant is the only solution.

THE LIVER: Vital statistics

- Your liver weighs about 3.5 pounds (1.6 kg)
- There are approximately 250 people on the UK's liver transplant waiting list at any one time
- Approximately 720 liver transplants are carried out in the UK every year
- In the 1970s, the early days of liver transplants, the survival rate was very low. But now the vast majority of the annual recipients of a new liver go on to lead healthy lives. According to UK Transplant, the five-year survival rate for adult liver transplants is 66%

mythbuster

The Myth: *Everyone with cirrhosis of the liver is an alcoholic.*

The Truth: Excessive alcohol is only one cause of liver damage – it can also be due to viruses, chemicals, diseases such as hepatitis, genetic diseases, problems with the immune system and also cryptogenic (that is, no known cause).

THE LIVER: How to live longer

■ Drink alcohol only in moderation – no more than 3 units daily for women, and 4 units for men

■ Don't take more than one medicine at once (this applies even to over-the-counter medicines) without checking with a pharmacist or your doctor. Drug interactions can produce chemicals that harm the liver as it tries to detoxify them

■ Cut down the amount of fat in your diet – it seems that a high-fat diet is linked with an increased risk of gall bladder disease

■ Drink moderate amounts of tea and coffee. Research suggests that some caffeine (between 2–3 cups of tea or coffee per day) can help protect the liver

■ If you're travelling to a country where hepatitis A or B are a risk, get vaccinated beforehand

■ Practice safe sex and don't use drugs. Hepatitis B and C can be spread through body fluids during sex, or via drug users sharing needles

CHAPTER 6

THE TURN BACK YOUR BODY CLOCK 8-WEEK EATING PLAN

eat to live longer

The foods we eat are implicated in the top 3 of the UK's 'big killers' – heart disease, stroke and cancer – so it stands to reason that good nutrition is one of the keys to living longer, and making sure those extra years are healthy and active ones. Poor diet is implicated in:

- Obesity
- High blood pressure
- Clogged arteries
- Heart disease
- Stroke
- Cancer
- Osteoporosis
- Diabetes
- Dental problems
- Osteoarthritis
- Fertility problems
- Poor immunity
- Digestive disorders
- Depression

A poor diet will take years off your death age. Your immune system will be dulled and you'll be more at risk from the diseases that could cut your life short, depriving you of precious years. In the meantime, your poorly nourished body and mind won't be able to enjoy the years you do have.

By fuelling your body with nutritious foods, you'll be able to squeeze out every potential day of your potential lifespan. And you'll be fit and healthy enough to enjoy it all.

Nutritionist Carina Norris devised the meal plans for participants in the Turn Back Your Body Clock television series. Her guidelines allow you to devise your own flexible longevity diet if you're less interested in losing weight than eating healthily.

Both the eating plan and the guidelines tick all the boxes for a 'longevity diet' as they'll reduce your risk of heart disease, stroke, diabetes, osteoporosis and cancer. They'll also give you tonnes of sustained energy and, of course, taste great.

The Turn Back Your Body Clock 8-Week Eating Plan provides you with slightly fewer calories than a 'weight-maintenance' eating plan, but it certainly isn't a crash diet. If you are overweight and you combine the menus with the Turn Back Your Body Clock exercise regime you will lose weight. But it will be a safe, slow, sustainable weight loss.

More importantly, the Turn Back Your Body Clock 8-Week Eating Plan is a longevity diet that concentrates on getting healthy nutrients inside you rather than cutting your calories. So you'll be well nourished and your general health will benefit.

- If you eat more fruit and vegetables you'll be eating more antioxidants, boosting your immune system, helping prevent your blood vessels from furring up and helping to protect yourself against cancer

- Starchy, high-fibre carbohydrates will sustain you between meals – there'll be no more gut-gnawing cravings for a chocolate biscuit – and provide vital B vitamins for your metabolism and your nervous system

- Low-fat protein will provide the building blocks for making cells for your new, healthy body

- Omega-3 and Omega-6 essential fatty acids from oily fish, nuts and seeds will boost your heart health, improve your skin and help keep your moods stable

- Dairy products, rich in calcium, will help protect your bones, and may also make you less likely to gain weight

You are not dieting to lose weight. You are eating to add years to your death age. Weight loss, if you need it, is a bonus.

longevity on a plate

The Turn Back Your Body Clock 8-Week Eating Plan will give you the knowledge to devise your own healthy and delicious way of eating; a diet that fits in with your own individual lifestyle. We're not going to ban your favourite food. If a chocolate bar every week helps you to stick to more nutritious foods the rest of the time, then go for it. Better to indulge once in a while than to deny yourself all treats, get resentful and miserable and then pack in 'this healthy eating lark' as a dead loss after two weeks because you can't have a chocolate fix.

A little of what you fancy does you good – in 'feel-good' terms at least. So there's no point denying yourself the foods you love, if it's going to make you miserable. If you limit yourself to the equivalent of, say, a good quality chocolate, or a couple of biscuits a day, you'll be fine. You want to splurge on a cream doughnut once in a while? It's okay, provided that you go easy on the days before and afterwards, so that your 'average' remains on target.

The same is true of an occasional glass of wine. As long as you stick within the recommended safe limits, you'll be fine. And if you want to go out for a celebration meal, enjoy yourself! Of course it makes sense to go for the healthier choices on the menu if you can, but don't beat yourself up if you go overboard once in a while. You can always be 'extra good' afterwards. Life is for living not dieting. But there have to be some rules. You must stick to the guidelines most of the time. It's all about getting the balance right. Armed with knowledge from the Turn Back Your Body Clock 8-Week Eating Plan, you'll know which foods are good for you and which aren't.

Making the
changes is
up to you

At least 3 portions of fruit a day – the more, the better

What to eat

A balanced diet for a healthy long life should contain roughly the following amounts of food per day:

Starchy foods	5–10 portions
Fruit	at least 3 portions a day – the more, the better
Vegetables	at least 3 portions a day – the more, the better
Protein foods	2–3 portions
Dairy foods	2–3 portions
Fatty and sugary treats	maximum 1 per day – try to do without!

Within those categories you've got a lot of choice, so you can tailor your diet towards the foods you like best. Here are just a few ideas…

A portion of starchy food

= a slice of wholemeal bread

= half a wholemeal bread roll, bagel or English muffin

= 1 medium baking potato, or the equivalent in smaller potatoes

= 3 rounded tablespoons cooked wholemeal pasta

= 2 tablespoons cooked brown rice

= 3 tablespoons low-sugar breakfast cereal

= 2 tablespoons no-sugar muesli

(Remember – potatoes count as starchy foods, not vegetables.)

A portion of fruit

= 1 slice of a large fruit (e.g. melon, pineapple)

= 1 medium fruit (e.g. apple, orange, banana)

= 2 small fruit (e.g. clementine, Satsuma, plum, kiwi fruit)

= 1 cup of berries, cherries, etc

= 3 tablespoons stewed fruit

= 1 tablespoon dried fruit (only once per day, as it's high in sugars)

A portion of vegetables

= approximately 80g vegetables (about 2 large tablespoons)

= a cereal bowl of salad

= one medium tomato (it's really a fruit, but most people think of tomatoes as vegetables)

A portion of protein

- = 100g meat or chicken
- = 125–175g (or a small tin) fish
- = 2 eggs
- = 4–5 tablespoons (or a small tin) beans
- = 50–90g tofu
- = 2 tablespoons nuts or seeds

A portion of dairy

Some dairy foods, such as milk and yoghurts, contain valuable amounts of protein, but they're given their own category for the purposes of this plan.

- = 200ml (a medium glass) of semi-skimmed or skimmed milk
- = 1 small pot (150g) low-fat yoghurt
- = 1 small carton (150g) low-fat cottage cheese

Try to include calcium-enriched soya milk, rice milk, yoghurt, etc., in your diet if you're dairy-intolerant or vegan.

Vegetarians can try tofu, which is a soybean curd and also Quorn® a meat substitute made from mushroom protein.

Things to do – NOW!

- Eat fish at least twice a week, making one of these servings (two if possible) an oily fish such as salmon, trout, sardines, pilchards or fresh tuna
- Eat a meal based around pulses (beans or lentils) at least three times a week
- If you do drink alcohol, stick to the safe recommended limits and try to avoid sugary liqueurs and alcopops

Tweaking the eating plan to suit you

If you find that you put on weight using these guidelines, tweak the portions a little. For example, cut back on snacks, lose some of the starchy food portions (limiting them to, say, 5 or 6 a day), make your pasta and rice portions slightly smaller, only have two rather than three protein and dairy portions a day, or reduce the size of the meat portions you have. If you're a big, active bloke who needs more calories and you're not trying to lose weight, then do the opposite. Just keep everything balanced and eventually you'll find what works for you.

How to make your choices healthy

- **Make it yourself.**
  - *Don't rely on ready meals and processed foods, and you'll instantly slash the fat, salt and sugar content of your meals. You'll also know exactly what goes into them*
- **Be kind to your protein.**
  - *Don't smother it in batter and deep-fry it, or douse it in creamy, fatty sauces*
- **Go for wholemeal.**
  - *Choose wholemeal bread, wholemeal pasta, brown rice, and other wholegrains such as buckwheat and bulgur. Refining grains to make them 'white' strips away the fibre, vitamins and minerals*
- **Eat the skins.**
  - *Eat potatoes in their jackets, don't peel your new potatoes and eat the skins of vegetables where you can. Scrub carrots and wipe mushrooms rather than peeling them. To avoid undue exposure to pesticides, go for organic options where you can afford them*
- **Reduce fat.**
  - *Cut down on the amount of fat you eat, and replace saturated fats (from animal products) with unsaturated fats (from vegetable oils). Avoid trans fats*
- **Go nuts!**
  - *Have a small handful of nuts or seeds (such as pumpkin or sunflower seeds) as a snack. They're relatively high in calories because of their oil content but they contain the heart-healthy mono- and poly-unsaturated oils that are good for you*

Getting started

If your current diet is a million miles from the Turn Back Your Body Clock 8-Week Eating plan, don't panic. Just ease in gradually.

- If you're not used to so much fruit, use it as a snack, replacing those sticky sweet things you used to reach for.
- Make sure that you have vegetables with both your lunch and dinner.
- Not used to so much dairy? Have skimmed milk as a drink with your meals. It won't block your nutrient absorption as tea and coffee do. Or have a mug of hot milk at bedtime.

Oily advice

When you need to use oil – for example a stir fry, brushing roast potatoes, tossing grilled Mediterranean vegetables, or brushing a piece of fish to grill – you don't need any more than 1 teaspoonful to 1 dessertspoonful per person. Use olive oil. Other oils can produce harmful free radicals when they're heated.

- Cut your portions of animal protein – a piece of meat the size of a pack of cards is a perfectly adequate serving.
- If you're used to having huge hunks of meat, cut down gradually so that you don't feel hard done by. Gradually decrease the meat serving size and replace it with other protein sources (such as pulses), grains or vegetables.
- Gradually switch to wholemeal bread. Try the various 'semi-wholemeal' breads available, wholemeal pasta, brown rice, and other wholegrains such as bulgur wheat, millet or buckwheat.

If you slip up, don't feel guilty. Just start again where you left off. You can have as many fresh starts as you like. Just don't give up! But remember: eat before you're ravenous, stop before you're stuffed.

Crash-free zone

The problem with crash diets is that they throw your metabolism out of kilter and confuse your body's natural weight-regulation systems. Because very low-calorie diets aren't enough to support a healthy body, not only can they make you deficient in vital nutrients, they also mean that dieters are hungry all the time. You become disconnected from the natural in-built urge to eat when you need food and stop when you've eaten all you need.

Also, on very low-calorie diets, your physiology switches to 'starvation mode', slowing down your metabolism because your body thinks there's a famine and it needs to store every calorie it can. This slows down your weight loss and if – or rather, when – you 'give up on the diet' the weight piles back on again.

And it now appears that this 'yo-yo' dieting is actually more dangerous, and knocks more years off your life, than being 'fat but fit'. It can also set up a cycle of despair, as each time you 'fail' you may feel less likely to succeed next time.

In contrast, a simple healthy-eating plan will help you to lose weight if you need to and maintain your weight if you're at your ideal weight already – provided that you are also keeping active.

Meal memos

Breakfast

- Try to get some fruit into your breakfast. It will help you reach your five-a-day fruit and vegetable target

- Complex carbohydrates – starchy foods, especially wholemeal – will help sustain you through the morning, so you don't give in to a sugary snack for elevenses

- Protein is your secret weapon in keeping you going and beating the mid-morning munchies – try breakfasts including protein foods like egg, baked beans or fish. Try salmon or sardines

Lunch and dinner

- Aim to cover half of your plate with vegetables

- Plus a portion of protein food – meat, fish, or a vegetarian alternative

- The rest of your plate is for starchy carbohydrates, such as potato, brown rice, wholemeal pasta, bulgur wheat, or wholemeal bread

the Turn Back Your Body Clock 8-week eating plan

So you want to fill up on the longevity nutrients that can add years to your life, and lose a bit of weight in the process? Here's the eating plan followed by the participants in the Turn Back Your Body Clock television series.

How to use the menu plans

You're going to follow the 4-week eating plan the participants used for the series, repeating the plan once.

Breakfasts

If you come to a breakfast you don't like, just substitute a breakfast from the same week. But try to eat a variety of breakfasts and not just your favourite one or two.

Lunches

If you come to a lunch you don't like, swap it for a similar lunch replacing red meat with red meat, chicken with chicken, etc.

Dinners

If you come to a dinner you don't like, you can swap one with the same main ingredient (fish, beans or lentils, etc.) For all meals, eat as many different dishes as you can rather than sticking to old favourites — variety is the key to getting all the nutrients you need. If you substitute lunches or dinners it is essential that you ensure that you still have:

- At least 2 servings of oily fish (tuna, salmon or sardines) and
- 1 serving of white fish every week
- No more than 2 dinners each week using red meat (beef, pork or lamb)

And make sure that you stick to the portion sizes.

Something for the weekend The lunches in the meal plan are designed as convenient packed lunches, but at the weekends feel free to swap your dinner with your lunch so that you have a cooked lunch and a cold, light meal in the evening. It is best not to eat a heavy meal late in the evening as your digestion slows down when you're sleeping.

Fruit, treats and desserts Each day you can have 2 additional portions of fruit (other than those listed as part of a meal) and fresh vegetable sticks at any time. You can also have 2 non-fruit snacks from the snacks list each day. On 2 days each week you may replace your non-fruit treats with a dessert from the desserts list. Don't forget to drink at least 1.5 litres of water each day.

MANSIZE ME!

The portion sizes in the Turn Back Your Body Clock 8-Week Eating Plan are for women. So here's the good news if you're a man. To enable you to get sufficient calories to keep you going during the day you should make the following changes:

- A portion of chicken or meat to be used in your dinner recipe should weigh approximately 150g. If you are having fish (no batter or crumb!) it should weigh 175–200g
- You should increase your dinner servings of pasta or rice by 10g (dry weight)
- When using boiled new potatoes you may have 150g (equivalent to about five small potatoes)
- At breakfast when having cereal increase this to 50g or alternatively add a slice of wholemeal toast
- Each day you may choose 3 items rather than 2 from the non-fruit snacks list
- On 2 days a week you may choose an item from the desserts list, without having to give up your snacks
- You may have 3 additional pieces of fruit each day and fresh vegetable sticks at any time

Non-fruit snacks

- 1 small low–fat natural yoghurt with 1tsp honey
- 1 small carton low-fat rice pudding
- 1 scoop fruit sorbet
- 2 digestive biscuits

- 1 currant bun with 1tsp low-sugar jam
- 1 slice malt loaf
- 1 cup of plain popcorn
- 2 squares of good-quality dark chocolate (70% cocoa solids or more)
- 1½ tbsp unsalted nuts and raisins
- 5 Brazil nuts
- 3 oatcakes, plain or spread with a teaspoon of honey or low-fat cream cheese
- 1 slice pumpernickel, spread with a teaspoon of low-fat cream cheese
- 2 rice cakes, with yeast extract or 1tsp reduced-sugar jam or honey

MAKE A NOTE OF IT:

General points before you get going

Don't skip meals, you'll just feel hungry and be tempted to snack. The snacks are optional not compulsory, so if you don't need them, leave them out.

You have an allowance of 300ml of skimmed milk for cereal and drinks throughout the day. Put the milk into a small jug at the beginning of each day and keep it in the fridge. Use the milk for cereals and drinks. If you have any milk left at the end of the day, drink it before going to bed – heat it up if you like.

A portion of chicken or meat to be used in a dinner recipe is 100g.

A portion of white fish is 150–175g.

A portion of oily fish is 100–150g.

Portions of pasta and rice are given as dry weight before cooking. If a portion size is not stated, use 40g dry/uncooked weight.

If not stated, a portion of boiled potatoes for a dinner is 100g or 3 small new potatoes. When you have mashed potatoes don't add butter – but you can use a splash of milk from your allowance.

A glass of pure fruit juice is 110ml.

Make sure you get wholemeal or granary bread – not just 'brown'. 'Brown' bread can in fact be white bread, just coloured brown.

See Appendices 2 and 3 for all the recipies in full (pp. 192–224)

week 1

DAY 1

Breakfast
1 medium egg scrambled on a toasted wholemeal English muffin
1 tomato cut in half and grilled
1 piece of fruit or glass of fruit juice

Lunch
Salmon and cucumber wholemeal sandwich
1 portion of fruit or raw vegetable sticks

Dinner
Jacket potato with curried bean filling
Large mixed salad

DAY 2

Breakfast
30g porridge oats cooked with water, then add 150ml skimmed milk,
    1 tbsp sultanas and drizzle with 1 tsp honey (optional)
1 slice wholemeal toast with a scraping of low-fat-spread and
    low-sugar jam or marmalade
1 piece of fruit or glass of fruit juice

Lunch
Wholemeal turkey and cranberry sandwich
1 portion of fruit or raw vegetable sticks

Dinner
Pan-fried cod
Boiled new potatoes and mixed fresh vegetables

DAY 3

Breakfast
1 egg omelette with a grilled tomato or some mushrooms and a slice
    of wholemeal toast
1 piece of fruit or glass of fruit juice

Lunch

Cottage cheese with pineapple, salad and crispbreads
1 portion of fruit or raw vegetable sticks

Dinner

Stir-fried beef with broccoli
Brown rice or noodles

DAY 4

Breakfast

3 tbsp fruit compote (apples, pears, peaches, prunes, etc.) stirred into
    a small tub of low-fat natural yoghurt, with 1 tbsp chopped nuts
1 slice wholemeal toast lightly spread with low-fat spread and
    low-sugar jam or marmalade
1 glass of fruit juice

Lunch

Egg and potato salad with wholemeal roll
1 portion of fruit or fresh vegetable sticks

Dinner

Spicy prawns and spaghetti
Large mixed salad

DAY 5

Breakfast

2 crumpets toasted and spread with a little low-fat soft cheese and
    yeast extract
1 piece of fruit or glass of fruit juice

Lunch

Tuna pasta salad made with 40g cooked pasta, ½ small tin tuna,
    and lots of chopped vegetables
1 portion of fruit or raw vegetable sticks

Dinner

Hot and sweet chicken
Boiled new potatoes, green beans and grilled or baked tomato

DAY 6

Breakfast

2 Weetabix or 30g cereal (low sugar and salt) with skimmed milk
1 small pot of low-fat fruit yoghurt
1 piece of fruit or glass of fruit juice

Lunch

Soft cheese, banana and runny honey on granary roll
1 portion of fruit or raw vegetable sticks

Dinner

Salmon and sweetcorn salad
Toasted crusty wholemeal roll

DAY 7

Breakfast

1 poached egg on a slice of wholemeal toast, lightly spread
   with a low-fat spread
6 mushrooms, halved and simmered in a saucepan with
   a little water or stock
1 piece of fruit or glass of fruit juice

Lunch

Grilled Mediterranean vegetables, feta cheese and salad leaves
   in a wrap
1 portion of fruit or raw vegetable sticks

Dinner

Speedy cheesy pasta
Green salad

week 2

DAY 1

Breakfast

2 Weetabix or 30g cereal (low sugar and salt)
1 small pot of low-fat fruit yoghurt
1 glass of fruit juice

Lunch

Soft cheese and carrot granary sandwich
1 portion of fruit or raw vegetable sticks

Dinner

Mustard chicken
Mixed salad or mixed fresh vegetables

DAY 2

Breakfast

1 small tin of no-added-sugar baked beans on a toasted wholemeal
    English muffin
1 medium tomato, halved and grilled
1 piece of fruit or glass of fruit juice

Lunch

Tuna and salad pitta
1 portion of fruit or raw vegetable sticks

Dinner

Simple vegetable and chickpea stew
New potatoes (or pasta) and green salad

DAY 3

Breakfast

Banana smoothie made with one sliced banana, 150ml skimmed milk,
    125ml low-fat natural or vanilla yoghurt
1 slice wholemeal toast spread with a little low-fat cream cheese,
    yeast extract or reduced-sugar marmalade

Lunch

Salmon (or tuna), sweetcorn and red or yellow pepper
   wholemeal sandwich
1 portion of fruit or raw vegetable sticks

Dinner

Grilled chicken breast with tomato and sweetcorn mash
Green beans and broccoli

DAY 4

Breakfast

8 prunes tinned in natural juice topped with a small tub of low-fat
   fromage frais
1 slice wholemeal toast lightly spread with a low-fat spread
   and low-sugar jam or marmalade
1 glass of fruit juice

Lunch

Ham and mustard sandwich on wholemeal submarine roll
1 portion of fruit or raw vegetable sticks

Dinner

Butter beans with mushrooms and cherry tomatoes
Mashed or boiled new potatoes and fresh vegetables

DAY 5

Breakfast

20g low-sugar cereal or muesli with 100g low-fat natural yoghurt
   and a piece of fresh fruit (or tinned fruit in natural juice)
1 glass of fruit juice

Lunch

Roast chicken with salad, coleslaw and granary roll
1 portion of fruit or raw vegetable sticks

Dinner

Crusty cod with cheese and tomato
Boiled new potatoes and fresh vegetables

DAY 6

Breakfast

2 Weetabix or 30g cereal (low sugar and salt)
1 small pot low-fat fruit yoghurt
Glass of pure fruit juice

Lunch

Cottage cheese with peach and salad, with 4 wholemeal crispbreads
1 portion of fruit or raw vegetable sticks

Dinner

Honey and mustard salmon
New potatoes, green beans and broccoli

DAY 7

Breakfast

Toasted sandwich made with a lightly boiled egg
1 halved grilled tomato
1 piece of fruit or glass of pure fruit juice

Lunch

Brown rice and vegetable salad with chicken, tuna or ham
1 portion of fruit or raw vegetable sticks

Dinner

Chickpea and vegetable chilli
Pasta and a mixed salad

week 3

DAY 1

Breakfast
1 medium egg scrambled on a toasted wholemeal English muffin
1 halved tomato, grilled
1 piece of fruit or glass of fruit juice

Lunch
Curried chicken wrap
1 portion of fruit or raw vegetable sticks

Dinner
Quick Balti fruity chicken curry
Brown rice and mixed salad

DAY 2

Breakfast
30g porridge oats cooked with water – then add 150ml skimmed milk,
   1 tbsp sultanas and 1 tsp honey (optional)
1 slice wholemeal toast lightly spread with a low-fat spread and
   low-sugar jam or marmalade
1 piece of fruit or glass of fruit juice

Lunch
Bagel with low-fat cream cheese and salmon and salad
1 portion of fruit or raw vegetable sticks

Dinner
Fresh tuna (or salmon) with lime and chilli
Boiled new potatoes or brown rice, and fresh vegetables

DAY 3

Breakfast
1 egg omelette with a grilled tomato or some mushrooms and a slice
   of wholemeal toast
1 piece of fruit or glass of fruit juice

Lunch

Small tin mackerel or sardines in tomato sauce, with salad in a
     granary roll
1 portion of fruit or raw vegetable sticks

Dinner

Spicy bean and lentil casserole
Green salad or fresh vegetables

DAY 4

Breakfast

3 tbsp fruit compote (apples, pears, peaches, prunes, etc.) stirred into
     a small tub of low-fat natural yoghurt with 1 tbsp chopped nuts
1 slice wholemeal toast lightly spread with a low-fat spread and
     low-sugar jam or marmalade
1 glass of fruit juice

Lunch

Nutty cheese pitta
1 portion of fruit or raw vegetable sticks

Dinner

Spicy lamb chop
Couscous and mixed salad

DAY 5

Breakfast

2 crumpets toasted and spread with a little low-fat soft cheese
     and Marmite (yeast extract)
1 piece of fruit or glass of fruit juice

Lunch

Light egg mayo on wholemeal submarine roll
1 portion of fruit or raw vegetable sticks

Dinner

Quick Mediterranean chicken casserole
New potatoes or pasta, and fresh vegetables

DAY 6

Breakfast

2 Weetabix or 30g cereal (low sugar and salt)
1 small pot low-fat fruit yoghurt
1 piece of fruit or glass of fruit juice

Lunch

Tuna, chopped tomato and watercress on wholemeal bread
1 portion of fruit or raw vegetable sticks

Dinner

Mushroom omelette
Baby boiled new potatoes, grilled tomatoes and sweetcorn

DAY 7

Breakfast

1 poached egg on a slice of wholemeal toast, lightly spread with a
    low-fat spread.
6 mushrooms, halved and simmered in a saucepan with a little water
    or stock
1 piece of fruit or glass of fruit juice

Lunch

Roast beef and horseradish sandwich, with tomato and salad leaves
    on wholemeal submarine roll
1 portion of fruit or raw vegetable sticks

Dinner

Speedy Oriental Quorn®
Brown rice

week 4

DAY 1

Breakfast

2 Weetabix or 30g cereal (low sugar and salt)
1 small pot low-fat fruit yoghurt
1 glass of fruit juice

Lunch

Tofu sausage and salad bowl
1 portion of fruit or raw vegetable sticks

Dinner

Spanish chicken
Pasta and green salad

DAY 2

Breakfast

1 small tin of no-added-sugar baked beans on a toasted wholemeal
   English muffin
1 halved grilled tomato
1 piece of fruit or glass of fruit juice

Lunch

Shredded chicken and salad bowl
1 portion of fruit or raw vegetable sticks

Dinner

Garlic and chilli prawn stir-fry
Wholemeal rice (or a crusty roll) and mixed salad

DAY 3

Breakfast

Banana Smoothie: using a blender, whiz together one sliced
banana, 150 ml skimmed milk, 125ml low-fat natural or vanilla
yoghurt. Pour into a tall glass. You can make this the night before
and keep in the fridge until morning.

1 slice wholemeal toast spread with a little low-fat cream cheese,
yeast extract or reduced-sugar marmalade

Lunch

Spicy stir-fried chicken and salad wrap
1 portion of fruit or raw vegetable sticks

Dinner

Spicy veggie burgers
Toasted wholemeal bap and salad

DAY 4

Breakfast

8 prunes tinned in natural juice with a small tub low-fat fromage frais
1 slice wholemeal toast lightly spread with a low-fat spread and
low-sugar jam or marmalade
1 glass of fruit juice

Lunch

Garlic cheese and salad wholemeal sandwich
1 portion of fruit or raw vegetable sticks

Dinner

Chicken with pepper salsa
Mixed green salad

DAY 5

Breakfast

20g low-sugar cereal or muesli with 100g low-fat natural yoghurt
and a piece of fresh fruit (or tinned fruit in natural juice) chopped
1 glass of fruit juice

Lunch

Salmon and cucumber wholemeal sandwich
1 portion of fruit or raw vegetable sticks

Dinner

Quick spicy sausage and beans
New potatoes or rice, and fresh vegetables

DAY 6

Breakfast

2 Weetabix or 30g cereal (low sugar and salt)
1 small pot low-fat fruit yoghurt
Glass of pure fruit juice

Lunch

Wholemeal turkey and cranberry sandwich
1 portion of fruit or raw vegetable sticks

Dinner

Grilled steak
Horseradish mash and mixed vegetables

DAY 7

Breakfast

1 lightly boiled egg in a toasted sandwich
1 halved grilled tomato
1 piece of fruit or glass of pure fruit juice

Lunch

Soft cheese and grated carrot granary sandwich
1 portion of fruit or raw vegetable sticks

Dinner

Vegetable and lentil stew
New potatoes or pasta, and green salad

See Appendices 2 and 3 (pp. 192-224) for all the recipes in full.

more energy, less waist = more years

If you kick-start your body with a cup of coffee and a muffin in the morning, or reach for a chocolate bar or handful of biscuits when you feel tired and munchy, you're making a rod for your own back. This kind of eating causes rollercoaster energy levels, so you keep on grabbing another sugary snack with the inevitable effect on your waistline – and your lifespan.

Sugary foods are quickly absorbed and metabolised by the body. They provide quick-release energy that certainly hits the spot (particularly when accompanied by the stimulant caffeine in coffee), but all too quickly they are used up, leaving you feeling sluggish once more.

The secret is to give your body slow-release fuel which sustains you between meals so that you don't resort to the quick-fix sugary snacks – that Danish pastry with a cappuccino on your way to work, the biscuits with morning coffee, or the mid-afternoon chocolate bar.

But foods such as starchy or 'complex' carbohydrates (particularly wholemeal versions), proteins and fats take longer for your body to absorb and process. The energy they provide is released slowly, rather than all at once, so they keep you going for longer.

This is the logic of the GI, or Glycaemic Index, principle. Slow-release, or low-GI foods, produce a slow but sustained rise in your blood sugar levels so that you don't get hungry between meals. They also help you to store glycogen in your muscles, an essential energy source for exercise. Quick-release, high-GI foods, produce a boom and bust rise and rapid fall in blood sugar levels, leaving you feeling weak, lethargic and craving another sugar hit.

Slow-fuel foods

So, what are these low-GI, 'slow fuel' foods that keep your energy levels nice and stable, avoiding the rollercoaster of high and low blood sugar associated with frequent sugar top-ups throughout the day?

Eating the low-GI way

■ Unprocessed, unrefined foods. Rather than white bread, pasta and rice, eat wholegrains, such as wholemeal bread, brown rice, brown pasta, and other grains such as oats, bulgur, millet and buckwheat. As well as removing the fibre and raising the GI, refining foods to make them 'white' also strips them of vitamins, especially the B vitamins which are vital to metabolise your food and release energy

■ Protein takes longer to digest than carbohydrate so your meal hangs around for longer in your stomach. This slows down the speed at which your blood sugar rises – it makes it a low-GI meal and beneficial 'slow fuel'

■ Fat also lingers in the stomach, therefore lowering a meal's GI. While it's not recommended that you add fat to your meals in order to sustain you for longer, a small amount of healthy mono-unsaturated olive oil, for example, can lower the GI of an otherwise high-GI food

■ Pulses – beans and lentils – are not just for hippies! These are some of the best low-GI foods, with both complex starchy carbohydrates and protein

■ Lightly boiled or steamed foods. Cooking starts the breakdown process that continues in your stomach – soft-cooked food takes less time to digest than foods that still have a little 'bite' to them. For example, crisp-tender steamed vegetables or pasta cooked 'al dente' has a better, lower GI, than if it's cooked until it's soggy. It's also more nutritious as there's less time for vitamins to escape into the cooking water

■ If you eat high-GI foods with low-GI foods, you get a medium-GI meal. So, if you must eat high-GI foods, such as the occasional sweet treat or white bread, make sure they're part of a meal that has a generally low GI. Don't eat them as a between-meal snack

GI and GL – what's the difference?

GL, or Glycaemic Load, is simply a more sophisticated extension of the GI principle, and it takes into account the amount of sugar contained in a portion of food, rather than just the speed with which that food raises your blood sugar levels. For example, carrots can be 'bad' under the GI philosophy because they have a high-GI score. But to get that high-GI effect, you'd have to eat buckets of carrots. GL considers just a normal portion of carrots – so with GL, carrots have a much more respectable score.

Get a wok. They're great for cooking quick and nutritious stir-fries

Turn Back cooking

The methods you use to cook your food can often determine whether the meal will be healthy or not. Ditch the frying pan and the deep-fat fryer – the most unhealthy options – for some of the more healthy cooking methods.

- Invest in a ridged griddle pan or electric health grill. They're ideal for cooking meat, poultry and fish and allow the fat to drain away
- Get a metal or bamboo steamer basket that fits in your saucepan, or an electric steamer. These are all perfect for steaming vegetables, poultry and fish, and you don't need to use any fat. You also avoid losing the water-soluble vitamins in the cooking water
- Use the grill on your cooker to cook vegetables such as mushrooms and tomatoes as well as fillets of fish, sardines, chicken breasts and lean, tender cuts of meat
- Oven-bake meat, poultry or fish by simply spraying the food lightly with olive oil, and cooking open or in foil parcels
- Get a wok. They're great for cooking quick and nutritious stir-fries using vegetables, meat, poultry, prawns or tofu chunks. You only need a tiny amount of oil

The Slow Food Movement

There was a time when we shopped locally, bought fresh produce almost daily and 'fast food' was just the ad man's dream. These days our eating is dominated by the food industry, especially the 'fast food' business. The Slow Food Movement was established in the 1980s by Italian Carlo Petrini when, to his horror, a brand-new fast-food restaurant opened at the foot of Rome's Spanish Steps. The movement has now spread around the world and advocates the opposite of fast food – food that's fresh, local and traceable to its source. The Slow Food Movement celebrates the heritage of local produce and the pleasure of eating tasty, authentic food.

Trim the fat

Many of us eat too much fat – we should get no more than 35% of our calories from fat, which works out as a maximum of 70g a day for women and 95g for men.

What to spread?

With such a wide variety of spreads available it's not surprising that we're often confused. So which should you choose? Look for spreads that say they are:

■ Low fat
■ Low in trans fats or preferably contain no trans fats
■ Low in saturates
■ High in poly-unsaturates or high in mono-unsaturates

Also check the ingredients list for hydrogenated and partially hydrogenated fats and oils, and avoid them whenever you can – if they contain these ingredients, they'll contain trans fats. Try a cholesterol-lowering spread – clinical trials have shown that these really do work.

Fat swaps

High fat	Lower fat
Red meat	Chicken and turkey (skin removed)
Sausages and pies	Fresh cuts of meat
Chips	Baked or boiled potatoes
Chicken curry with pilau rice	Chicken tikka with salad
Whole milk	Semi-skimmed or skimmed milk
Full-fat yoghurt	Low-fat yoghurt
Full fat cheese (e.g. Cheddar, Stilton)	Half-fat hard cheese (e.g. mozzarella, feta)
Ice cream	Frozen yoghurt or sorbet
Crisps	Savoury rice cakes or rice crackers
Peanuts	Twiglets

CHAPTER 7

THE BIG C

everything you need to know about cancer

Cancer is a scary disease, but because so many cases are linked to your lifestyle – nutrition, obesity, smoking, drinking – there's a lot you can do to minimise your risk.

Dr Una says...

Cancers begin when the DNA in one of your 10 trillion cells is damaged, causing a mutation. Normally, the body is able to repair the problem or the cell when the damaged DNA commits suicide, but if it doesn't the mutated cell containing the cancer-causing gene, or oncogene, lives on and spreads throughout your body and may also be passed on to your children (inherited cancers).

Only if these two natural defence mechanisms fail do problems result and the cell's natural division process spins out of control, forming a tumour. Some tumours are harmless (benign) lumps, but others become malignant, or cancerous. These grow and invade neighbouring tissues, causing pain and damage and stopping organs and tissues from working properly. Sometimes cancerous cells can break off and be carried to distant parts of the body in the bloodstream or lymphatic system, where they can seed new, secondary tumours.

Most cancers develop slowly and they may have been growing undetected for some time before they're diagnosed. Although cancer does occur in children, it's much more common the older you get. Causes of cancer include:

- Poor diet
- Obesity
- Smoking
- Alcohol
- Sun exposure
- Environmental pollution
- Asbestos
- Radiation
- Certain viruses linked to liver, stomach and cervical cancer, and leukaemia
- Benzene

Everyone has the tumour suppressor gene p53, which protects you from getting cancer. It has now been proven that the tar in cigarette smoke contains BPDE (benzoapyrinediolepoxide) a toxic subtance that damages your tumour suppressor gene. If this gene is switched off you can develop cancer anywhere in your body.

Secondary or side-stream smoke is more lethal than primary or mainstream smoke. Side-stream smoke comes from the burning end of the cigarette and is inhaled without a filter. Cigarette smoke contains tar (cancer-causing), carbon monoxide (displaced oxygen from your blood) and nicotine.

Things that increase your risk:

- Age (the older you are)
- Inheriting a gene or genes associated with cancer
- Having a weak immune system (for example, people with HIV or who are taking immunosuppressive drugs after an organ transplant)

CANCER: Vital statistics

- Cancer is the number 2 killer in the UK
- 26% of deaths in the UK are caused by cancer
- There are over 200 kinds of cancer
- Lung, breast, bowel and prostate cancers account for around 50% of cancer cases in the UK
- 30–40% of cancers may be caused by poor diet
- Approximately 30% of cancers may be caused by smoking
- The younger you start to smoke, the greater the risk of cancer
- The World Health Organisation estimates 15 million new cases of cancer each year due to increased smoking in developing nations, and poor diets

The Myth: *If you've got a 'cancer gene' from your parents you're bound to develop the disease.*

The Truth: Genetics can make you more prone to developing cancer but it's rare for an inherited mutation to actually cause the disease – there usually has to be a trigger too.

The ten most common cancers in women

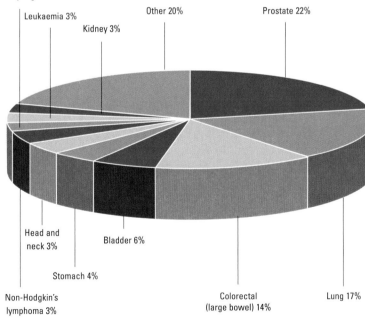

Stomach 2%

Other 25%

Breast 30%

Bladder 2%

Pancreas 3%

Melanoma 3%

Uterus 4%

Non-Hodgkin's lymphoma 3%

Ovary 5%

Lung 11%

Colorectal (large bowel) 12%

The ten most common cancers in men

Oesophagus 3%

Leukaemia 3%

Kidney 3%

Other 20%

Prostate 22%

Head and neck 3%

Bladder 6%

Stomach 4%

Non-Hodgkin's lymphoma 3%

Colorectal (large bowel) 14%

Lung 17%

(UK incidence 2001) Source: Cancer Research UK 2005

CANCER: How to live longer

TURN BACK YOUR BODY CLOCK

Maintain a healthy weight

Take exercise – it's been found to decrease your cancer risk

Reduce your fat intake, especially saturated and trans fats

Reduce your salt intake

Eat more fruit and vegetables

Eat more fibre

Don't eat food cooked using methods that involve charring

Limit your intake of smoked or salty foods – they can increase your risk of stomach cancer

Drink alcohol only in moderation

Don't smoke

Don't overexpose yourself to the sun

Try to avoid harmful chemicals and pollutants

Take advantage of any cancer-screening services you may be eligible for. Ask at your GP's practice for information

BOWEL CANCER: How to live longer

Eat plenty of fibre, found in fruit, vegetables, wholegrains and pulses.

■ *Fibre speeds the passage of waste products through the bowel, limiting the amount of time potential carcinogens (cancer-causing chemicals) spend in contact with the bowel wall*

■ *Fibre also ferments in the bowel, producing butyrate, a cancer-inhibiting chemical*

Eat lots of brassica vegetables – cabbage, broccoli, cauliflower, Brussels sprouts, etc. They contain phytochemicals (plant chemicals) called isothiocyanates which are thought to help protect against bowel cancer

Reduce your fat intake, especially from processed and red meat. These kinds of meat are linked with an increased bowel cancer risk

Maintain a healthy weight

Take regular exercise

BOWEL CANCER

Bowel cancer can occur anywhere from the back passage to the colon (large intestine or bowel). There are various risk factors:

■ Family or personal history of bowel cancer
■ Previous history of ulcerative colitis or Crohn's disease
■ Age – the older you are, the greater your risk
■ Unhealthy diet (high in fat and red meat, and low in fruit, vegetables and fibre)
■ Smoking
■ Obesity

BOWEL CANCER: Vital statistics

■ In terms of numbers, colon cancer kills the equivalent of a jumbo jet crash per week
■ Second most common cause of cancer deaths
■ Third most commonly occurring cancer in the UK
■ 9 out of 10 people who develop bowel cancer are over 50
■ Average age at diagnosis is 65
■ Curable in 40–50% of cases. The earlier it's detected the better your chances of survival

Dr Una's 10 warning signs of cancer

1 A solitary lump in the breast or elsewhere, especially if it keeps growing in size
2 A sore that does not heal in the mouth or elsewhere after 3 weeks
3 Change in bladder habits (painless blood in the urine)
4 Change in bowel habits (persistent constipation, diarrhoea, or fresh blood in the stool)
5 Changes to a mole (bleeding, colour change, irregular edges or itchiness
6 Difficulty swallowing or persistent indigestion
7 Nagging cough for more than 2 weeks, especially in a smoker
8 Postmenopausal bleeding from the vagina
9 Unexplained bleeding or discharge from the mouth, nipple, nose, or skin
10 Unexplained weight loss in a short period of time

Dr Una's top 10 tips to preventing cancer

1 Avoid smoky areas where you can be exposed to secondary smoke, and don't smoke
2 Bald men should wear hats when in the sun to avoid skin cancer
3 Check your breasts for lumps while in the bath or shower, particularly if you are between 50 and 64, the age group most at risk for breast cancer. Early detection is vital for optimum treatment and extended lifespan
4 Get your breasts checked with mammograms between the ages of 50 and 64
5 Keep your Pap smears up-to-date to allow early detection of cervical cancer
6 Wear sunscreen with an SPF of at least 15 and avoid the sun in the afternoon between 12p.m. and 3p.m. to prevent skin cancer
7 Diets high in saturated fats and red meat are linked with cancer, so limit high-fat foods, especially from animals
8 Lack of fruit and vegetables in the diet cause cancer, so eat 5 portions of fruit and veg a day
9 Maintain a normal weight. Obesity is linked to colon, gallbladder, prostate, kidney, postmenopausal breast cancer and womb cancer
10 Limit your alcohol intake

BREAST CANCER: How to live longer

The good news is that thanks to earlier detection and better treatment the death rate from breast cancer in the UK has fallen by a fifth in the last ten years. To help reduce your risk you need to:

Watch your weight

Exercise and keep fit. A large-scale study found that women who walked briskly for an hour a day had a 20% less risk of breast cancer

Don't eat too much fat, and concentrate on 'good fats'

Eat plenty of fruit and veg

Fill up on fibre-rich foods such as wholegrains and pulses

Don't exceed the safe limits for alcohol

Be breast aware, and examine your breasts – see if your doctor's surgery offers a Well Woman Clinic or ask your practice nurse

If you have babies, breast-feed them if possible.

After the age of 50 you can ask your doctor to refer you for a mammogram. If there is breast cancer in your family, you may be eligible for earlier screening

BREAST CANCER

According to a survey by the British Lung Foundation, breast cancer is the disease women in the UK fear the most. Risk factors for breast cancer are:

- Age. It's more likely the older you are
- HRT and the contraceptive pill. Both are thought to increase your risk slightly, but this appears to return to normal after you stop taking them
- Genetics. Breast cancer can run in families
- Starting your periods early
- Late menopause
- Being overweight after the menopause

Be breast aware – TLC for breasts

Breakthrough Breast Cancer recommends that you give your breasts TLC:

T is for Touch	TOUCH your breasts. Feel for anything unusual
L is for Look	LOOK for changes. Be aware of their shape and texture
C is for Check	CHECK anything unusual with your doctor. Chat with your friends if you are worried

BREAST CANCER: Vital statistics

- Breast cancer is the most common cancer for women in the UK
- It accounts for 1 in 3 female cancer cases
- 1 in 9 women will develop breast cancer during their lifetime
- About 80% per cent of women diagnosed are over 50 and half of those are over 60
- 1 in 20 cases of breast cancer are caused by an inherited gene
- Men can get breast cancer too – but only 300 are diagnosed each year, compared with 41,000 women

CERVICAL CANCER

Cervical cancer is hard to detect in its early stages and it's often not caught until it's advanced. This cancer develops in the cells lining the cervix – the canal connecting the uterus (womb) to the vagina. It can then spread to other parts of the body such as the uterus, vagina or bowel.

Cervical cancer develops slowly. Often the first stage is the appearance of so-called 'abnormal cells'. Sometimes, but not always, these go on to develop into cancerous cells. The key to successful treatment is catching the disease early. If doctors can detect pre-cancerous changes they can initiate treatment and stop the cancer from developing. There are various risk factors.

- A sexually transmitted infection called human papillomavirus (HPV). Some high-risk types of HPV can cause abnormalities in the cells in the cervix, which develop into cervical cancer. Most women with cervical cancer are infected with high-risk HPV, but not all women with the virus go on to develop the cancer. In fact, most sexually active women are infected with HPV – it's that common
- Sexual behaviour. Being sexually active at an early age and having many sexual partners increases your risk of cervical cancer by increasing your potential exposure to the human papillomavirus. Using condoms could help to reduce the risk of infection
- Smoking. Smoking can as much as double your risk of cervical cancer
- Weakened immune system. People whose immune system is suppressed (perhaps by HIV, or by taking immunosuppressant drugs for a medical condition) may be less able to fight off the human papillomavirus

CERVICAL CANCER: Vital statistics

- Every year, 3,000 women are diagnosed with cervical cancer in the UK
- It's the second most common cancer in women aged under 35
- Cervical screening saves the lives of thousands of women each year

CERVICAL CANCER: How to live longer

Have a regular cervical smear test. Your GP's surgery should call you for one every 3–5 years between the ages of 25 and 64. Screening helps doctors to detect abnormal cells before they have the chance to develop into cancer cells

Quit smoking

Cervical cancer often produces no symptoms. In the vast majority of cases potential symptoms are in fact due to some other, more minor, complaint. But it's better to be safe than sorry, so you should see your doctor if you notice any of the following:

- *Bleeding between periods*
- *Bleeding after sex*
- *Bleeding after you've gone through the menopause*
- *An unusual vaginal discharge*
- *Painful sex*

LUNG CANCER: How to live longer

Stop smoking. See pp. 54-6 for advice on quitting. You'll also take incentive from the other ways that smoking can knock years off your life

Avoid smoky rooms where possible – you can also get lung cancer by passive smoking

Eat plenty of antioxidant-rich fruit and vegetables, which can help protect you from cancer

LUNG CANCER

Lung cancer is a particularly deadly form of cancer – only liver, pancreatic and pleural cancers are more deadly. Because the symptoms are often mild at first, and are easy to put down to other causes (such as a cough), the disease often isn't diagnosed until it's well advanced.

Lung cancer is notoriously difficult to treat and, by the time it's diagnosed, often the most doctors can do is relieve the patient's symptoms for as long as possible.

LUNG CANCER: Vital statistics

- Lung cancer is the most common cancer in the world
- In the UK it is the second most common cancer in men and the third most common in women
- Lung cancer causes 20% of all UK cancer deaths
- It kills approximately 40,000 people every year in the UK
- 75% of people who die from lung cancer are over 65
- Only about 10% of people diagnosed with lung cancer are 'cured', that is, they are still alive with no signs of the disease five years later
- 90% of lung cancers are caused by smoking
- The rest are caused by industrial chemicals such as asbestos, or radon gas

PROSTATE CANCER

Prostate cancer is the commonest male cancer. Tumours tend to form around the edges of the prostate gland and it is easy for cancer cells to break off and spread to other parts of the body, particularly the bones.

Although it's very rare in men under 45, and is generally very slow-growing, sometimes men develop an aggressive form of the cancer, which grows quickly.

The symptoms of prostate cancer include having to rush to the toilet to urinate, difficulty starting or stopping urinating, pain on urination, blood in the urine or semen, or pain in the lower back or hips.

Many of these symptoms can be caused by the normal age-related enlargement of the prostate or a non-cancerous condition called benign prostatic hyperplasia. So, if you notice any of the symptoms, you should go to your doctor. If prostate cancer is detected early, recovery chances are fairly good.

PROSTATE CANCER: Vital statistics

- **30,000 men in the UK are diagnosed with prostate cancer every year**
- **Every year, approximately 10,000 men in the UK die of the disease**
- **The lifetime risk for men to develop prostate cancer in the UK is 1 in 14**
- **Vegetarians are half as likely to develop prostate cancer as meat eaters**

PROSTATE CANCER: How to live longer

Eat plenty of fruit, vegetables, nuts and seeds for their anti-cancer antioxidants

Eat lots of tomatoes. They contain a phytochemical called lycopene which helps protect against prostate cancer. Cooked tomatoes (including tinned tomatoes and even tomato ketchup – low sugar, please) are the best sources of lycopene

Eat selenium-rich foods such as Brazil nuts, fish, wholegrains, eggs and garlic. Studies strongly suggest that the mineral selenium is highly protective against prostate cancer, both helping to prevent cancers from starting and slowing the progress of prostate cancer if it has already developed

Decrease your meat intake. Population studies suggest that vegetarians have a lower risk of prostate cancer

Take plenty of exercise. Studies suggest it decreases your risk of prostate cancer

TURN
BACK
YOUR BODY CLOCK

The good news is that 80% of cases of skin cancer are preventable by practising 'safe sun'.

Keep the skin covered up as much as possible in the sun

Always use a sunscreen of at least SPF 15 on exposed areas of the body

Don't allow your skin to burn

Reapply sunscreen frequently

Children under three should be kept out of the sun at all times. Older children should wear an SPF 30 on exposed areas of the body

Seek shade between 11a.m. and 3p.m.

Avoid using sunbeds

SKIN CANCER

Skin cancer occurs when skin cells grow out of control, often spreading to other parts of the body to cause secondary cancers. It's caused by exposure to the sun's ultraviolet (UV) rays and the risk increases after sunburn, particularly if this happens in childhood. The damage – and also the risk – builds up over the years. Although people who are exposed to a lot of sun during childhood can develop skin cancer in their twenties and thirties, the disease is generally diagnosed in much older people.

You don't have to roast yourself on foreign beaches to increase your risk, either. Skiers are just as vulnerable because the UV rays are reflected off the snow. And swimmers in the sea can be burned by UV rays reflecting off the water. Even in a generally dreary climate like the UK's, on a sunny day you can still burn in 10 minutes.

Add to this the fact that the damaged ozone layer lets through more UV rays, and the increasing popularity of sunbeds (which use UV light), it's easy to see why so many people develop this cancer.

It's hard to judge whether a skin cancer has developed because of sunbed use, but a recent scientific study estimated that UVA sunbeds might account for about 6% of melanoma deaths each year in the UK.

People with naturally dark skin, such as Hispanic and African-Caribbean people, are less likely to develop skin cancer than fairer skinned people. They are afforded natural protection against UV rays by the melanin pigment in their skin. People with fair skin, red hair or freckles are most at risk.

SKIN CANCER: Vital statistics

- Skin cancer is the most common cancer in the UK. Over 69,000 new cases are registered in the UK every year
- More than 2,000 people die of the disease annually in the UK
- Malignant melanoma (the more serious form of skin cancer) makes up only 10% of skin cancers, but 80% of skin cancer deaths
- Twice as many women as men are diagnosed with skin cancer
- The commonest site of skin cancer is the lower legs in women, and the chest and back in men

- Although malignant melanoma is most common in the over forties, among people under 35 it is the third most common cancer in women and the sixth most common in men.

There are three main kinds of skin cancer.

Basal cell carcinoma and squamous cell carcinoma

These are the most common skin cancers and, with about 62,000 new cases diagnosed each year, among the most common kinds of cancers in the UK. Basal cell carcinoma affects the cells at the lower end of the epidermis, which is the top layer of the skin. Squamous cell carcinoma affects the cells closest to the skin's surface. These kinds of cancer usually appear as scaly, eczema-like patches of skin.

Malignant melanoma (or melanoma)

Melanoma is also known as 'mole cancer' as it generally develops from a mole. This cancer is less common, with about 7,000 new cases of malignant melanoma being detected every year. But it is the most deadly type of skin cancer and it's increasing at an alarming rate in the UK. Incidence has more than doubled in the last 20 years. Survival depends on early detection and treatment.

Be mole aware

Keep an eye on your moles. Danger signs to look for include any moles that are:

- Getting larger
- Changing shape, particularly if their edge is becoming ragged or irregular
- Changing colour – for example getting darker, patchy or multi-shaded (moles come in all colours, from yellowish through orange and shades of brown and black, and even greenish and bluish)
- Itchy or painful
- Bleeding or crusty
- Inflamed

Your doctor can take a sample from your worrisome mole so that it can be tested for cancer cells.

the immune system

Your immune system is your body's defence against disease. Without it, you'd be a goner! Your body is under constant attack from millions of viruses, bacteria and allergens such as pollen and dust, but – most of the time – your immune system fights them off. Problems arise when your immune system isn't up to scratch. Germs can slip through your defences, causing illnesses ranging from the common cold to life-threatening diseases like meningitis. Your immune system is also part of your defence against cancer. So it stands to reason that you ought to do all you can to strengthen your immune system and anything that weakens it is a bad thing.

THE IMMUNE SYSTEM: How to live longer

Certain things will weaken your immune system and need to be avoided.

- *Poor nutrition. If you have a malnourished body you will have a weakened immune system*

- *Stress. Think how students often go down with colds and flu before and during exam time, or how performers start sniffling before a show*

- *Not enough, or too much, exercise. Both lack of activity, and overexerting yourself, can weaken your immune system*

free radicals

Free radicals are highly reactive molecules that can cause no end of trouble. They're formed when an oxygen molecule loses an electron, making it very unstable. To regain stability, the free radical snatches an electron from another molecule, which in turn becomes a free radical and produces a chain reaction. Free radicals are bad news. By grabbing electrons from other molecules they cause 'oxidative damage' in various parts of the body:

- In the arteries. They encourage atherosclerosis or the 'furring up' that increases your risk of heart disease and stroke

- In the joints. They cause inflammation, which can lead to pain and arthritis

- In the DNA of cells anywhere in the body, making you more prone to developing cancer

- In the eye. They can cause macular degeneration, a major cause of blindness in those over 60

- In the brain – which can make you more likely to develop disorders such as Parkinson's or Alzheimer's disease

- In the skin. They lead to a loss of elasticity, which encourages wrinkles

In fact free radical damage is thought to be behind the ageing process itself, so it stands to reason that in order to live longer you should protect yourself from these harmful molecules. You can't avoid exposure to free radicals – not least because they're also produced by normal processes in the body, like when you metabolise your food. But they're also produced by UV sunlight, cigarette smoke, air pollution and charred and fried food. And these are things that can be avoided.

Things to do – NOW!

Quit smoking, and avoid smoky places

Avoid traffic fumes where possible – wear a mask if you're cycling or jogging near traffic

Avoid overexposure to the sun – wear a sunscreen, and don't let yourself get burned

Don't eat food that's been charred (e.g. burnt barbecue food, or chargrilled food)

Minimise your intake of fried foods

Don't reuse frying oil – this is a dead cert way of making free radicals

FREE RADICALS: How to live longer

You have a defence against dangerous free radicals in the form of natural food chemicals called antioxidants. These can 'mop up' and neutralise free radicals before they cause any harm. Antioxidants 'donate' electrons to replace those that the free radicals have lost. And because antioxidants are stable, with or without the donated electron, they don't become harmful free radicals themselves. Antioxidants are found in a variety of healthy foods – fruit and vegetables are a brilliant source. There are many kinds of antioxidants. Here are just a few:

- Vitamins, such as the 'ACE' vitamins – vitamins A, C and E. Get vitamin A from liver, oily fish and eggs. Get vitamin C from fruit and vegetables, especially kiwi fruit and citrus fruit. Get vitamin E from nuts and seeds and their oils

- Some minerals – such as selenium, found in Brazil nuts, shellfish, kidney and liver

- Carotenoids – such as beta-carotene and lycopene, found in yellow, orange and red fruits and vegetables

- Anthocyanins – pigments found in red and purple fruits such as blueberries, cherries and red grapes

- Catechins – found in green and black tea, and dark chocolate

- Polyphenols – found in dark chocolate and red wine

the top 10 superfoods

1 **Garlic.** Studies suggest that garlic can reduce your risk of heart attack and stroke by making the blood less sticky and less likely to clot. It can also help reduce high blood pressure and high blood cholesterol levels. Allicin, the compound that gives garlic its characteristic smell and taste, acts as a powerful antibiotic and also has antiviral and antifungal properties.

2 **Carrots.** Carrots are super-rich in beta-carotene, which the body converts to vitamin A – important for healthy eyes, skin and a strong immune system. Eating a beta-carotene-rich diet helps protect against certain types of cancer.

3 **Tomatoes.** Tomatoes are a good source of the natural plant chemical (phytochemical) lycopene, which helps protect against cancers, especially prostate cancer. They are packed with antioxidants including vitamins C and E, plus beta-carotene. These help protect the body from free radicals – oxygen molecules that can damage the body's cells.

4 **Olive oil.** Olive oil is a heart-healthy unsaturated fat, which can help lower your levels of the 'bad' LDL cholesterol that contributes to clogged arteries, heart disease and stroke. It's also a good source of the antioxidant vitamin E.

5 **Brazil nuts.** Brazil nuts are a supreme source of the mineral selenium, which helps support the immune system. They're packed with protein, and although high in fat, it's fat of the healthy mono-unsaturated and poly-unsaturated varieties.

6 **Oats.** Oats are rich in soluble fibre that can help reduce levels of the 'bad' LDL type of cholesterol, lowering your risk of heart disease and stroke. Oats are a low-GI food, which means they'll help regulate blood sugar levels and you'll feel full for longer. They're also a useful source of protein, B vitamins, calcium and magnesium.

7 **Kiwi fruit.** Weight for weight, kiwi fruit are twice as rich in the powerful antioxidant vitamin C as oranges. Just one little kiwi provides twice your recommended minimum intake for the day. Vitamin C helps support the immune system, protecting you from infection and diseases such as cancer. Vitamin C-rich foods can also enhance your absorption of iron. Kiwi fruits are also a good source of potassium, which helps regulate fluid levels and blood pressure.

8 **Salmon.** Salmon is rich in Omega-3 fatty acids, which help to keep the cardiovascular system healthy by lowering your levels of 'bad' LDL cholesterol and raising your levels of 'good' HDL cholesterol. Omega-3s can also help keep your brain healthy.

9 **Pumpkin seeds.** Pumpkin seeds are a great source of the mineral zinc, essential for a healthy immune system. Zinc is also needed for a healthy reproductive system. They're also a good source of protein, B-complex vitamins, and essential fatty acids.

10 **Broccoli.** Broccoli is a great source of carotenoids, which protect your immune system. Broccoli, and other members of the cabbage family, contain phytochemicals called glucosinolates. They help protect against cancer, particularly bowel cancer. Broccoli is also a valuable source of iron, folic acid and vitamin C.

Easy ways to put your superfoods to work

■ Add fresh crushed or chopped garlic late in your cooking to get the best health benefits. If you like the strong taste, add it raw to salads, salad dressings and dips

■ Don't cook your carrots to death – raw or crisp-tender is best. Steam if possible and, if you boil, don't add salt to the cooking water. Add grated carrots to salads and to sandwich fillings. Grated carrot is delicious with a low-oil dressing, chopped walnuts and sultanas

■ Unlike many other vegetables, cooking tomatoes makes their nutrients more available to the body. Cherry tomatoes are even richer in nutrients than their larger relatives. Use tomatoes – tinned are just as good – in pasta sauces, pizza toppings, stews and casseroles

■ Brush olive oil on to meat and fish before grilling. Use a small quantity to oil a pan before frying. Use it to make salad dressings

- Use two or three Brazil nuts as a snack with some raisins. Chop them up and add to your breakfast cereal or to a cold dessert

- There's a porridge for everyone, so don't give up on oats if you have bad memories from your childhood. For a smooth, comforting breakfast or snack, try 'instant oats' (avoid the sweetened versions) or fine oatmeal. Then there's porridge oats, medium or coarse oatmeal, or jumbo oats for more texture. For a really nutty bite, try pinhead or steel-cut oatmeal

- Make your own crunchy fish fingers or chicken nuggets by dipping fish or chicken pieces in beaten egg, then in seasoned porridge oats. Bake in the oven

- Kiwi fruits are ideal for lunchboxes and healthy snacks. Just cut one in half and eat it with a teaspoon like a hard-boiled egg. Top yoghurt and muesli with a sliced kiwi fruit for a tasty breakfast or dessert

- Eat the soft, cooked bones of tinned salmon along with the flesh – they're rich in calcium, which is essential for healthy bones. Combine with mashed potatoes and fresh parsley to make speedy fish cakes. Grill salmon fillets, sprinkle with sweet chilli dipping sauce and serve on a bed of watercress

- Use pumpkin seeds as a snack with raisins. Chop them up and add them to crumble toppings. You can also add them to breakfast cereals

- Steam rather than boil your broccoli. If you boil it and throw away the cooking water, you lose much of the water-soluble vitamins. Slice the florets and add to stir-fries

the truth about organic food

Organic food is undeniably more expensive than conventionally produced food – but is it worth it if the extra cost is adding years to your life?

The Soil Association says that eating a predominantly organic diet can:

- Reduce the amount of toxic chemicals you take in with your food
- Reduce your intake of food additives and colourings
- Increase your intake of vitamins, minerals, essential fatty acids and antioxidants
- Have the potential to lower the incidence of common conditions such as cancer, coronary heart disease, allergies and hyperactivity in children

What you avoid if you go organic

- Pesticides
  - *UK Government research has consistently found pesticide residues in a third of foods, including apples, baby food, bread, cereal bars, fresh salmon, lemons, lettuces, peaches, nectarines, potatoes and strawberries*
  - *The 'cocktail effect' – eating a combination of pesticides – could be even more harmful than you'd expect, because of complex chemical interactions*
- Food additives.
  - *Approximately 300 additives are allowed in conventional food, but only 30 are permitted under the Soil Association's organic standards*
  - *Just some of the potential nasties not allowed in organic food include the flavour enhancer monosodium glutamate, the sweetener aspartame, and phosphoric acid*
- Trans fats.
  - *Food with a Soil Association organic label isn't allowed to contain trans fats*

- **Genetically Modified Organisms.**
  - *The long-term effects of GMOs on health are as yet unknown. You may object to being a human guinea pig*

Organic food can contain more…
- **Vitamins and minerals.**
  - *The Soil Association compared the vitamin and mineral content of organic and conventionally grown food and found that organic food contains higher levels of vitamin C, calcium, magnesium, iron and chromium. Organic spinach, lettuce, cabbage and potatoes were particularly good for minerals*
- **Phytochemicals (plant chemicals).**
  - *Phytochemicals have a whole host of health benefits, including protecting against heart disease and cancer. Many phytochemicals are also powerful antioxidants and mop up harmful free radicals in the body.*
- **Antioxidants.**
  - *Antioxidants can reduce your risk of clogged arteries, high blood pressure, heart disease, stroke and cancer*
  - *Danish research has concluded that organic crops contain 10% –50% more antioxidants than conventional crops.*
- **Essential fatty acids.**
  - *Organic milk and beef appears to be higher in Omega-3 fatty acids than conventionally produced milk and beef*

ORGANIC FOOD: Vital statistics

- **Women with breast cancer are 5–9 times more likely to have pesticide residues in their blood than women without breast cancer**

- **In a study of pre-school children in Canada, youngsters eating conventionally farmed fruit and vegetables had levels of pesticides up to 6 times higher than those who ate organically. Because of their smaller body sizes and developing bodies, pesticides could be even more harmful to children than to adults**

metabolic syndrome

Not many people have heard of Metabolic Syndrome, but far too many suffer from it. It is also called Insulin Resistance Syndrome, or Syndrome X. While not a 'disease' itself, Metabolic Syndrome is a cluster of symptoms that work together to lop years off your life by clogging your arteries and increasing your risk of Type 2 diabetes and cardiovascular disease (heart attack and stroke).

METABOLIC SYNDROME: How to live longer

Maintain a healthy weight

Minimise your intake of saturated and trans fats

Replace some of your saturated and trans fats with mono- and poly-unsaturated oils, especially the Omega-3s from oily fish

Cut down on salt

Eat plenty of fruit and vegetables, for artery-protecting antioxidants

Exercise – at least 30 minutes moderate exercise 5 or more days a week

Have your blood pressure and cholesterol levels checked regularly, especially if you have any of the other Metabolic Syndrome symptoms or if there's cardiovascular disease or diabetes in your family

Having just one of the symptoms lowers your chances of living out your full potential lifespan, but the nastiest thing about Metabolic Syndrome is the way the combined effect of two or more symptoms multiply together to increase the risk of an early death.

And because all of the symptoms are linked, you commonly find them together.

Insulin resistance occurs when the body does not respond properly to insulin, the blood sugar-regulating hormone, even though there's plenty of insulin in the bloodstream. At its most severe, insulin resistance leads to Type 2 Diabetes. You're generally considered to have Metabolic Syndrome if you have three of the symptoms below.

- Obesity – especially around the middle (central obesity or 'apple shape')
- High blood pressure
- High blood triglycerides (lipids or fats) and low levels of the 'good' HDL cholesterol
- Insulin resistance

diabetes

Diabetes occurs when the body cannot produce enough, or even any, of the blood sugar control hormone, insulin. It can reduce your death age and your quality of life. It can:

- Raise blood pressure and blood lipid (fat) and cholesterol levels, increasing the risk of heart disease and stroke
- Lead to kidney disease
- Lead to cataracts
- Lead to nerve damage of the extremities
- Increase the risk of suffering from gout, a painful joint condition

Dr Una says...

When you suffer from diabetes you cannot regulate your blood sugar levels. Normally, after a meal, your blood glucose level rises, which triggers the body to produce insulin. This then shuttles the glucose into your body's cells where it can be used or stored. In diabetes there is a problem with the insulin system, and blood sugar (blood glucose) levels remain too high.

There are two main kinds of diabetes – Types 1 and 2:

Type 1 diabetes This generally arises in children or young people, when the insulin-producing cells of the pancreas are destroyed. Type 1 diabetes is generally called an 'auto-immune' disease, where the body attacks itself, killing off the pancreas cells. The usual treatment is insulin injections.

Type 2 diabetes This used to be called 'adult onset diabetes' because it was rare in people under 40. But now, thanks largely to unhealthy lifestyles, it's being seen in younger people, and even children. It occurs when the pancreas doesn't produce enough insulin, or the body doesn't respond properly to the hormone even though plenty is being produced. Type 2 diabetes can often be controlled with diet and tablets, though sometimes insulin injections are needed.

The Myth: *Eating too much sugar will give you diabetes.*

The Truth: It's your body weight that puts you at risk. Sugar can help you put on weight, but it's not the only culprit.

DIABETES: How to live longer

There's plenty you can do to reduce your risk of Type 2 diabetes.

Make sure you're not overweight or obese

Take enough exercise

Keep an eye on your blood pressure, blood cholesterol and waist measurement – if they're high you could have Metabolic Syndrome

Reduce your total fat intake, and eat moderate amounts of 'good' mono- and poly-unsaturated fats

Reduce the amount of processed and fast food you eat

Cut back on salt

Consult yout doctor if you show symptoms of the condition

There are various risk factors:
- Being over 40 years old
- Being Asian or Afro-Caribbean
- A family history of Type 2 diabetes
- Being overweight or obese
- Metabolic Syndrome
- Giving birth to a large baby
- A cholesterol reading of more than 5 mmol

Detecting diabetes

Symptoms include tiredness, weight loss, being thirsty all the time, wanting to pass urine very frequently and suffering from vaginal and anal itchiness. With Type 1 diabetes, the symptoms generally develop over a few weeks, but the onset is much slower in Type 2 and generally the initial symptoms are much more mild, so it's often only detected during routine blood tests.

DIABETES: Vital statistics

- Approximately 1.6 million people in the UK have been diagnosed with diabetes
- This many again may have Type 2 diabetes but not know it
  Over the last 30 years, cases of childhood diabetes have tripled
- Type 2 diabetes is much more common than Type 1, making up 90% of cases
- Men with Type 2 diabetes have approximately three times the risk of coronary heart disease. For women with Type 2 diabetes the risk of coronary heart disease increases fourfold
- More than 25,000 people with diabetes die of cardiovascular disease (heart attack and stroke) every year

sugar: naughty or nice?

In a healthy diet, sugary foods are high on the list of foods to avoid. Sugar can cause you to gain weight (though in fact it's not as calorific as alcohol or fat) because it's so more-ish. And you often find it combined with fat in favourites like cakes, chocolate, biscuits, pastries, etc. It's a lethal combination for your waistline.

Refined sugars also cause a rapid rise in blood sugar levels, giving you that instant energy rush that soon disappears, leaving you hungry again and often craving more sugar. And on top of that, sugar spells disaster for your teeth – particularly when you eat it between meals. But there's no such thing as a totally 'bad' food and sugars are no exception. It's a question of how much sugar you eat, and what kinds.

It's recommended you eat no more than 12 teaspoons of sugar a day – and that isn't just the sugar we add to drinks or sprinkle on strawberries. Unfortunately most of us are unaware of just how much sugar we consume as a lot is hidden in processed foods like cakes and biscuits, tinned foods and breakfast cereals – even the non sugar-coated ones. You'll also find a surprising amount lurking in tinned foods such as spaghetti, baked beans and vegetables. The secret is to learn to read labels and learn to recognise sugar in its many guises so that you can choose the low-sugar options.

Sugars often end in 'ose' so look out for:

- Sucrose
- Glucose
- Fructose
- Lactose
- Maltose
- Dextrose
- Treacle
- Honey
- Golden syrup
- Corn syrup
- Maple syrup
- Invert sugar
- Raw sugar
- Hydrolysed starch

Natural sugars are contained in some fresh foods. For example, fruit contains fructose, and milk contains lactose. These sugars are less quickly absorbed by the body and sustain you for longer. These natural sugars also come 'packaged' with a range of other essential nutrients like protein, vitamins, minerals, phytochemicals and fibre. Because of these linked healthy benefits, these natural sugars aren't included in your 12-teaspoons-per-day recommended limit.

Limit your sugar intake

Don't eat sugary foods between meals – the frequency of sugar eating is more important than the actual quantity in determining the harm to your teeth

Clean your teeth at least twice a day, and preferably after eating sugary foods as well

Avoid fizzy drinks, even sugar-free ones, as they're still acidic and can erode your teeth

Floss daily

Have regular dental check-ups

Hang on to your teeth

Keeping your teeth and gums in good shape could lessen your risk of a heart attack or stroke. Researchers have found that people with gum disease (periodonitis) are almost twice as likely to suffer from coronary artery disease as those without gum disease. Gum disease involves pockets of bacterial infection in the gums. Sometimes this infection slips over into the bloodstream, where it can cause inflammation of the artery walls. These inflamed areas can then act as 'starter areas', which make the arteries more likely to 'fur up', restricting the blood flow and increasing the likelihood of heart disease and stroke. Gum disease – and the bacteria in the bloodstream – can also make existing heart conditions worse.

Reinforcing the link between bad gums and heart disease, scientists have also shown that gum disease increases the level of a protein in the blood called C-reactive protein (CRP). The significance? High levels of CRP are an even more accurate indicator of heart attack risk than high cholesterol levels.

Things to do – NOW!

Change to low-sugar cereals for breakfast and reduced-sugar jams and marmalades, tinned spaghetti and baked beans. Chutneys and pickles may also contain a lot more sugar than you'd expect, and so can products labelled 'low fat' – manufacturers take out the fat and then pile in the sugar to make them taste good. Get into the habit of baking your own cakes and biscuits. That way you can reduce the amount of sugar you add to recipes. Experiment, and you'll often find that you don't need as much as the recipe says, particularly if there are other ingredients providing sweetness, like dried fruit, or fresh fruit such as apple or mashed bananas.

A can of fizzy drink can contain 10 teaspoons of sugar

stroke

A stroke is a 'brain attack'. It occurs when a blood vessel in the brain bleeds or is blocked by a blood clot. This leads to an area of brain cells being starved of oxygenated blood so that those cells die. There are two kinds of stroke:

STROKE: How to live longer

Quit smoking, and avoid smoky rooms if you're a non-smoker

Maintain a healthy weight

Replace some of the saturated and trans fats in your diet with healthier mono- and poly-unsaturated fats

Cut down on salt – eat no more than 6g per day

De-stress – practise relaxation

Drink sensibly – eat no more than the recommended limit of alcohol

Take exercise. It's good for your blood pressure and helps prevent your arteries from becoming clogged

Have your blood pressure and cholesterol levels checked regularly, especially if you have a family history of atherosclerosis

Ischaemic stroke

This is the 'blood clot' type of stroke, and its main cause is atherosclerosis – clogged arteries. A clot may form in the blood vessels to the brain or it may form elsewhere in the body and then be carried around the blood system and become lodged in one of the brain's blood vessels.

Haemorrhagic stroke

This is the 'bleed' type of stroke, caused when a brain blood vessel ruptures at a weak spot. Sometimes it's caused by a weakness in the blood vessel (an aneurysm) that was present from birth, but it can also be due to a head injury, an infection, or a blood-clotting disorder.

STROKE: Vital statistics

- Stroke is the third biggest killer in the UK – that's 100,000 strokes every year
- Every five minutes someone in the UK has a stroke
- Stroke is the main cause of disability in the UK – 300,000 people live with stroke-related disability
- 9 out of 10 strokes affect those over 55
- After a first stroke, a third of people recover well, a third become disabled and a third die within a year
- 40% of strokes could be prevented by lifestyle changes such as giving up smoking

osteoporosis

Osteoporosis means that your bones become porous and brittle. A small bump, or even just a lot of pressure, can cause a fracture. You might ask 'what's so deadly about a fracture?' but broken bones, and the complications that can arise, are a significant cause of death in the elderly. Broken bones can also lead to loss of mobility. If you're less able or unable to exercise and your general fitness, heart and lung function and muscle strength and tone suffer, you increase your risk of cardiovascular disease. The problem with osteoporosis is that you can't feel your bones thinning. The first thing you'll notice is a loss of height – as your weakened spine begins to curve under your own weight – or a fracture after a minor knock.

Dr Una says...

Bones are made up of a mesh formed by a protein called collagen, combined with minerals (mainly calcium). The outer regions of bone are dense, while the inner regions contain the bone marrow, blood vessels and nerves, set in a less dense honeycomb of protein and minerals. Bone is constantly being broken down and recycled. When you're young, you build up more bone than you break down, achieving maximum bone density in your mid-twenties. For about 10 years, bone formation keeps pace with bone breakdown, so your bone density remains the same. But from your mid-thirties onwards, you begin to break down more bone than you build, so your bones gradually become weaker as you grow older. The dense outer layer becomes thinner and the 'holes' in the inner honeycomb become larger.

18% of people suffering a hip fracture die in the following three months

14,000 people die each year in the UK following a hip fracture

Some things speed the process of bone thinning, increasing your risk of osteoporosis:

- In women, lack of the female hormone oestrogen
    - *For example, after the menopause*
    - *Women whose periods stop for more than six months, other than during pregnancy. This is usually caused by low body weight and low body fat, and can be the result of eating disorders or the lifestyle demands associated with being a professional dancer or sportswoman*
- In men, lack of the male hormone testosterone
- Family history of osteoporosis
- Long-term use of high-dose steroid drugs (perhaps for asthma)
- Lack of activity
- Smoking
- Excessive drinking

OSTEOPOROSIS: Vital statistics
- Approximately 3 million people in the UK suffer from osteoporosis
- 50% of women and 20% of men will suffer a fracture after the age of 50
- Every 3 minutes someone has a fracture caused by osteoporosis
    - *Each year there are more than 230,000 fractures, including more than 50,000 wrist fractures, 70,000 hip fractures and 120,000 spinal fractures*
- Osteoporosis costs the UK over £1.7 billion each year – or £5 million each day
- For women, the 1 in 6 risk of sustaining a hip fracture is greater than the 1 in 9 risk of developing breast cancer

OSTEOPOROSIS: How to live longer

Bone thinning is an unavoidable part of the natural ageing process. But you can minimise your risk of osteoporosis by building up as much bone as you can during childhood and in your twenties and thirties, and doing everything possible to minimise bone breakdown after that. Because the gradual decline of bone density begins when we're so young – in our thirties – it's particularly important to pay all we can into our 'bone bank' as soon as possible. But you can help your bones at any age by following these points:

- Calcium is needed for building bone, so eat plenty of dairy products, an excellent source
- Other good calcium sources include:
  - *Tinned fish where the soft bones are eaten, such as salmon and sardines, as well as baked beans, tofu, sesame seeds, dried apricots and green leafy vegetables like kale*
- Vitamin D is needed for the body to use calcium.
  - *The body can produce some of its own vitamin D from the effect of sunlight on the skin. Fifteen minutes' sun exposure is enough – you don't need to sunbathe*
  - *You can also get it from oily fish (such as salmon, mackerel, sardines and tuna), meat, eggs and dairy products*
- Do weight-bearing exercise, like walking, running, skipping or tennis. It needn't be high impact, and 20 minutes a day is enough.
- If you smoke, quit
- Drink alcohol only in moderation
- Minimise your caffeine intake. There is some evidence that drinks containing caffeine, such as coffee and cola, can cause excess excretion of calcium from the body
- Avoid fizzy drinks. Phosphoric acid contained in many fizzy drinks can hinder calcium uptake from food
- After the menopause, certain hormone replacement therapy (specifically a drug called raloxifene) may reduce your risk of osteoporosis. But HRT is not for everyone. There can be side effects and it can increase your risk of other diseases – so you need to discuss this with your doctor to weigh up the pros and cons
- After the menopause, take a calcium supplement such as Calcichew (calcium plus vitamin D). This is especially important if you're naturally small-framed

osteoporosis: are you at risk?

To help you bone up on your osteoporosis, try this quiz. It's aimed mainly at women as the osteoporosis risk for women is much higher than for men. But men can do it too. Just score zero for any question that's obviously one for the girls!

1 How old are you?
[0]   Under 40
[1]   41–55
[5]   56–75
[10] 76+

2 Is there any parental history of osteoporosis?
[2]   Yes
[0]   No

3 What about your build?
[2]   Naturally slim
[1]   Medium
[0]   Big boned

4 Have your periods ever stopped for more than 6 months, other than during pregnancy or after the menopause (for example, due to an eating disorder, weight loss or athletic training)?
[2]   Yes
[0]   No

5 Did you have an early menopause (that is, before the age of 45)?
[3]   Yes
[0]   No
[0]   I am under 45

6 Did you have an early hysterectomy (that is, before the age of 45)?
[3]   Yes
[0]   No
[0]   I am under 45

7 Have you taken corticosteroid medication (perhaps for asthma) for 5 years or more?
[3]   Yes
[0]   No

8 Do you drink more than the recommended alcohol limit (14 units per week for women, 21 for men)?
[2]   Yes
[0]   No

9 Do you smoke?
[0]   No
[1]   Yes – 10 or fewer a day
[2]   Yes – more than 10 a day

10 How active are you, in work and everyday life?
[1]   Not very active
[0]   Very active

11 Do you do any weight-bearing exercise, such as walking, jogging or running for 20 minutes or more twice a week?

[0]   Yes

[3]   No

12 Does your skin get 15 minutes or more of sun exposure every day?

[0]   Yes

[1]   No

13 How much dairy products or calcium-fortified dairy products do you have each day?

[1]   Less than 400ml

[0]   More than 400ml

14 How many portions of tinned fish where the bones are eaten (salmon, sardines, etc.) do you have a week?

[0]   Two or more

[1]   Less than this

15 If you have passed the menopause, do you take a calcium and vitamin D supplement?

[0]   Yes

[2]   No

[0]   I have not reached the menopause

Now add up your score:

9–13: Medium risk of osteoporosis.

8 or under: Low risk of osteoporosis.

If you scored 14 or more, or gained a non-zero score for questions 4, 5 or 6: You should certainly talk to your doctor about your osteoporosis risk – she may want to refer you for a bone-density scan.

get supported

Family, friends, hugs and prayers make the world go around, and also help you to live longer. Research has found that people who have a close social network around them are less likely to be depressed, stressed or pessimistic. And, more to the point, they tend to live longer.

On the purely practical side of things, if you have people to turn to they can look after you and help you recover after an illness or injury, or offer you help and advice about money, work or relationships. But the benefits go deeper than that – simply knowing that you have friends and people who care makes you feel more content and at ease with life. It lowers your stress levels, helping to keep your blood pressure nice and low and your immunity good and strong. It also makes you feel happier and more optimistic – a personality trait associated with people who live a long time. And the icing on the cake is that going out to meet people helps keep your body and mind active.

So it makes good sense to foster your relationships with your family, friends, work colleagues, the people you meet at church, at sports clubs, hobby groups, doing volunteer work or attending college classes. They can help you to manage stress, boost your morale and self-esteem when you're feeling low and help you take a 'rosier' view of life. Your social network will support you when you are sick, when the boss is giving you a hard time or if you are having an emotional crisis … and you are there to do the same for others.

Helping others has emotional benefits for you as well. People who attend church regularly and those who pray have been found to have a larger than average social network to support them.

But it is not only through the difficult times that your friends and family are there for you, they are there to share the good times as well. Women often find it easier to build and sustain wider social networks than men. Psychologists believe that this is because men are more competitive than women. When men are involved in sports they are often more intent on beating the other team than becoming friends with them. Women, on the other hand, are likely to want to get to know their opponents and invite them out for coffee.

If you are lucky enough to have a happy and settled personal relationship then you have got something to celebrate. Being happily attached keeps you healthy, as well as providing companionship, love and support.

You can't overestimate the power of friends, so if you think your social network is missing some links, it's time to get out there and meet new people. Remember a social network is a two-way road: the more you invest in it the more you will get out of it.

> *An Australian study found that elderly people with the firmest network of friends had a 22% lower chance of dying in the next 10 years.*

Is your glass half empty or half full?

If your answer is 'half empty' then it's time to try to cultivate some optimism. Optimists live longer than their pessimistic cousins, according to many scientific studies. They're healthier, have more vitality, make friends more easily and enjoy life.

- Smile when you meet someone
- Meditate or just relax in a quite place for ten minutes every day
- Call a friend
- Take a walk in the country
- Go out for lunch
- Laugh out loud. Watch a funny movie, or read a humorous book
- Make time every day to do something you enjoy, even if it's just relaxing in a hot bath filled with bubbles
- Give the garden a good going over

test your support system

1 Do you live in a happy relationship
with a partner?
[1] No
[3] Yes

2 Do you share accommodation with a friend?
[1] No
[2] Yes

3 Do you have family members living within
20 minutes travelling distance?
[1] No
[2] Yes

4 How often do you visit friends and family?
[1] Infrequently
[3] Frequently

5 If you are unable to visit family members
because of distance, do you keep in touch
by email, phone or letters?
[1] Infrequently
[2] Frequently

6 Do you have a network of friends with whom
you socialise regularly?
[1] No
[2] Yes

7 Do you regularly socialise with work
colleagues outside of work?
[1] No
[2] Yes

8 Do you take part in a physical activity
that involves meeting people at least once
a week?
[1] No
[2] Yes

9 Do you have a hobby or pastime that
involves meeting other people?
[1] No
[2] Yes

10 Do you attend any form of religious
meetings?
[1] No
[2] Yes

11 Are you involved in any voluntary or
charitable work?
[1] No
[2] Yes

Now add up your score:

11–14: You don't have much of a social support network – try to interact with people more, and build up your relationships.

15–20: Your social support network is helping you a lot, but increasing it could add years to your life.

21–25: You have an excellent social support network. Well done and keep it up!

pets – a prescription for good health

Medical experts acknowledge that a pet can play a positive part in your well-being. Studies have shown that not only do they help keep you fit and active, they can lower your blood pressure, have measurable effects on recovery after a heart attack and even help you to resist the common cold.

As you get older, pets can bring a wide range of benefits. An animal companion can alleviate loneliness and isolation and provide a sense of security, making us less likely to succumb to depression. Providing for a pet's day-to-day needs – feeding, grooming, exercise – boosts an elderly person's self-esteem and gives them a sense of feeling 'needed'.

Pet-owning pensioners also have higher levels of activity and exercise – with obvious implications for their longevity, by lowering their risk of heart disease, stroke and cancer. Walking a dog allows them social contact with the 'outside world' – and we've already mentioned how meeting people and making friends can help you live longer. Even caring for and playing with a cat can help.

While it's long been known that stroking a cat or dog can reduce your feelings of stress, loneliness and boredom, a study in the 1990s at the Baker Medical Institute in Australia showed that keeping a pet also significantly reduces cholesterol, blood triglycerides (fats) and blood pressure – thereby lowering some of the risk factors associated with heart disease. A mid-1990s study at Brooklyn College, New York, revealed that, of 369 patients who suffered a heart attack, pet owners were approximately 6% more likely to be alive in one year than those without pets. This may seem a small improvement in the survival rate, but given that nearly 114,000 people die of heart disease in the UK every year it could mean nearly 7,000 extra heart patients surviving thanks – at least in part – to their pets.

Scientists also believe that children who grow up in pet-owning households are less likely to suffer from minor infections than those in non-pet households. It's thought that the constant 'low-grade' stimulation of the immune system by antigens from the pets keeps their immune system on its toes. Children have also been found to be less likely to develop allergies (and this includes all allergies, not just allergies to pets) in pet-owning households. Striving for a virtually sterile environment is now believed to be counter-productive in trying to prevent allergies and illness – in adults as well as children. Sensible hygiene is of course crucial, but not wrapping yourself and your family up in cotton wool is the wisest course of action.

There are a few diseases that you can catch from your pet, but in general good hygiene – always washing your hands thoroughly after handling your pet – is all you need to prevent problems.

- *Some people may be allergic to cats or dogs*
- *If you are pregnant or have suppressed immunity you should assign cleaning the cat's litter tray to someone else*

CHAPTER 9

HOW TO EXERCISE

let's get physical

Food is only part of the longevity story. You also need to get active. Physical activity is vital in helping to:

- Lower your proportion of body fat, and increase your proportion of body muscle
- Aid weight loss, when combined with a healthy diet
- Give you more energy and stamina
- Lower your blood pressure
- Reduce your risk of heart disease by lowering your cholesterol level
- Lower your risk of certain types of cancer
- Reduce your risk of diabetes
- Improve bone density (depending on the type of exercise), therefore reducing your risk of osteoporosis
- Improve your quality of life, especially as you grow older

But exercise isn't just for the body, it also helps your mind. Exercise stimulates the production of endorphins – 'happy' chemicals that make you feel exhilarated and motivated. So exercise is not only good for you … it makes you feel happy. And that can't be bad.

Exercise adds years

Using data gathered over 46 years from 5,000 people, American scientists concluded that men who regularly engaged in high levels of physical activity live on average 3.7 years longer than their slothful cousins, and active women live 3.5 years longer. Even people engaging in moderate physical activity (such as power walking) added an average of 1.3 years to their lifespan.

EXERCISE: Vital statistics

- The United States attributes 12% of total deaths to lack of exercise
- The Department of Health estimates that lack of physical activity costs the UK economy £8.2 billion per year in terms of costs to the Health Service plus lost productivity through workers being ill
- Only 37% of men and 24% of women do the recommended amount of exercise – that's at least 30 minutes of moderate activity, five or more days a week
- The latest government survey found that only 51% of men and 36% of women had taken part in any sports activities (including walking) in the previous month
- The most popular exercise activities in the UK are:
  - *Walking*
  - *Swimming*
  - *Fitness classes/yoga*
  - *Cycling*
- For every 3,500 calories you burn off with exercise, you'll shed a pound. 3,500 calories sounds a lot, but all you need to do is use up an extra 300 calories a day through activity while reducing your dietary intake by 200 calories per day. By the end of a week you'll have a negative calorie balance of 3,500, which equates to a 1lb weight loss

A Swedish study published in the journal Lancet Neurology suggests that as little as two 30-minute exercise sessions a week could cut your risk of Alzheimer's by 50%.

EXERCISE: How to live longer

If you have a chronic health problem such as obesity, heart problems, diabetes, bone or joint disorders, if you're a smoker or are pregnant, you should check with your doctor before beginning an exercise programme.

But if you're merely a total couch potato, be inspired by the fact that you're going to benefit most from even a tiny increase in your activity levels. The health benefits of rising from zero to one on the fitness scale are far greater than increasing from a super-fit nine to a ten. Even introducing a little gentle walking into your routine will improve your fitness and stamina. Once this becomes easy, just pick up the pace or increase the distance.

Each year millions of pounds are spent on weight loss and dieting to lose body fat. There are few success stories. Research shows that three out of four adults don't exercise enough and are overweight. While you may understand that lack of exercise can lead to fat accumulation, you may not understand why. You know you're gaining fat, but perhaps you don't realise that you are also losing muscle. And muscle loss is a major factor in fat gain! If you knew this you might not place such an emphasis on dieting.

With one out of every two adults presently following a reduced-calorie diet plan, there needs to be a major teaching effort from health and fitness professionals to remedy this situation. Although dieting can reduce fat, it cannot replace muscle to solve the primary body composition problem.

Even people who don't increase their food intake experience creeping obesity as they get older because calories previously used to maintain muscle tissue are now being placed in fat-storage areas of the body.

There's no miracle solution. Physiologically, the problem doesn't occur overnight. It takes years of imbalances and neglect, or indeed confusion. The only realistic way to make long-term beneficial changes is to understand how your body works.

A common strategy for quick weight loss is to cut calories. But during periods of restricted food intake your hormonal activity slows your basal metabolic rate – the number of calories you use when you're resting and your body is just ticking over – to compensate for the reduced calorie intake and to ensure your survival.

Advertising claims of weight losses up to 3 kg (6.6lb) per week without exercise are extremely misleading. The majority of these losses are not fat at all but are mostly losses of carbohydrate and water stores.

The downside of this is that when your body is deprived of its carbohydrate stores your concentration, physical and mental function suffer, but you have not yet touched on much of your stored fats. This explains why you may experience a plateau early on in your diet and feel excessively tired, frustrated and depressed.

And, of course, when you return to your old eating habits you gain weight again because your metabolic rate had dropped to compensate for your low calorie intake.

How high your metabolic rate is, or how fast you burn calories, is governed by the amount of muscle you have, as muscle is constantly active tissue. Men burn more calories at rest than women merely because they have a higher density of muscle tissue. Although it's hormonally active, fat is inert as a calorie burner. This means that losses to lean body mass (muscle) through calorie restriction will lower the metabolic rate again and predispose a dieter to further and faster fat gain.

If you are under stress, go for a hard run at your gym

You need to differentiate between weight loss and fat loss. For good health and body shape it's the fat that needs reducing rather than carbohydrate, water or muscle. And as you now know, making drastic cuts to your energy intake can lower your resting metabolic rate and also reduce the general amount of calories you burn.

You need to understand that, for the most part, the problem of too much weight is really a problem of too little of the right type of exercise.

This means that an exercise programme must include strength training to replace muscle and restore your resting metabolic rate. There's no short-term solution to fat loss. Increasing activity should form part of a permanent lifestyle change.

Things to do – NOW!

- **Start lifting weights. In as little as 8 weeks you can permanently raise your resting metabolic rate by 20%**
- **Start running. Running burns the most energy and it will get you fitter quicker. And fit people burn fat faster**
- **If you're under stress, go for a hard run or head for the weights room at your gym. Exercising at moderate to heavy intensity triggers the release of the 'feel good' endorphins from the brain. These give you that sense of well-being that helps eliminate stress and dampens the urge to overeat**

Getting Started

Physique Expert Tim Bean, who devised the exercise plans for the Turn Back Your Body Clock television series, says that the success of any regime is a gym-based training programme as it is crucial to have access to a good range of commercial weight-lifting equipment in order to achieve the expected results. And no, women do not bulk up simply from lifting weights – their muscle tone improves and shape is enhanced.

You'll also find most clubs have a vast array of indoor cardio equipment and many classes to try out if exercising in a group is what motivates you.

The best times for training are first thing in the morning, in a lunch hour, or on the way home from work. So first you need to find a suitable club. You need one that's convenient and accessible. It must have good parking if you require it and be handy either to your home or to your work. If you have to go out of your way to make the trip there it's less likely that you'll bother when you're tired, rushed or distracted.

The next thing is to check that your chosen club is clean. Check there's no mould around the changing room showers and that the toilet seats and bowls are spotless. Make sure there are no sweat marks left on the upholstery or machine consoles in the gym itself.

Lastly, assess if the training areas are comfortable and functional. Look to see if there's enough room in and around the machines for your personal space and to move around safely. Check that there's adequate ventilation and the air-conditioning is working. Ensure there are drink stations or water fountains available in the training areas. Read the sign that says: 'Gym Rules and Etiquette', and see if anyone's following or enforcing them. Look for an instructor. There should be an instructor supervising the training areas at all times. This should be someone who is not involved in conducting personal training sessions with clients, or performing a fitness assessment in another room. They should be both present and available.

Once you've decided on a club, the next job is to find a trainer to help you get your programme under way. Ask the club's membership advisor – the person who showed you around on your first 'tour' – who they would recommend and why. Most clubs insist their trainers are qualified, so what you're looking for is experience and a track record of getting results. All trainers are not equal, so here are some things to look for:

- Most good trainers are heavily booked, and be warned they may be more expensive

- The most successful trainers will have a folder with testimonials and records of their successful training programmes with other people. Ask to see it. Ask if it's okay to talk to a couple of their past clients. You're looking for success in getting results, professionalism versus over-familiarity, with punctuality and strong leadership skills

- Check that their area of expertise is what you're looking for (for example, weight loss, athletics, running, body-building, etc.) and that their presentation matches your expectations of this. If, for example, weight loss or improving your physique is your prime goal then don't hire a trainer who's carrying any excess weight. Their expertise clearly lies elsewhere

■ All good trainers have a training log system to record and monitor progress with all your workouts

■ A good trainer will insist you get a full assessment and measure-up before you start, and will be keen to give you regular monthly assessments. This is good for accurately tracking your results, and is a sign of a competent and confident trainer – money well spent

■ Ask if the club provides some sort of starter pack of 3 or 4 sessions with a trainer at a special rate to get you started. This will ensure you get the right advice and instruction on a programme, as well as allowing you to assess if you actually get on well at a personal level with the trainer. Sometimes you will be encouraged to commit to a 10 or 20 session pack, which may not be a good idea to start with. However, once you've tested the waters, it's a great way to stay committed and on track

Choosing a club: Tim's essential questions
■ *Is its location convenient?*
■ *Is it open when you want it to be?*
■ *Is it clean?*
■ *Is the training area comfortable and functional?*
■ *Is the equipment well maintained?*
■ *Are the trainers up to standard?*
■ *Do you get on with them?*
■ *Is there a minimum contract, or can you sign up for a shorter series of 'taster sessions'?*

the 8-week plan

Tim says:

'For the participants in the Turn Back Your Body Clock television series I devised an 8-week plan, splitting the programme into 2 phases of 4 weeks each. Most important in the first 4 weeks is to get your muscles tuned up, as better muscle equals more calories burned. You also need to build up your joint strength and tensile strength in the muscle in preparation for the second 4 weeks, where there is more aerobic work. You don't want to break down from injury or strains.'

PHASE 1

3 days per week Work with your trainer to create a routine that should only take about 30–40 minutes to complete (including rests between sets), and can be followed by 20 minutes of cardio (aerobic) work if you have excess energy.

2 days per week On two other days you need about 30–40 minutes of straight cardio exercise. If you're really unfit this could be a power walk in the park (or on the treadmill/elliptical trainer in the gym if the weather is too bad or it's too dark for safety). If you're already quite fit you could be taking a Bodystep®, body conditioning, Body Attack® or spinning class, or running if you can get outside. This can be built up to 60 minutes per session as and when your fitness improves.

PHASE 2

Now you drop one day of gym training in the weights room and substitute some more cardio training. By now you should be able to complete a full 60 minutes of cardio training without stopping. You also have the option to increase this to 4 times a week for a better, faster result if time permits.

The workout

Your trainer is in the best position to prescribe the most appropriate routine for your individual condition. However you'll need a workout that includes exercises that target mainly the large muscle groups. These exercises are usually quite demanding and include multiple joint actions.

All these are ideal:
- **Squats**
- **Lunges**
- **Rows**
- **Presses**

These will involve a combination of machines, cable equipment and free weights (bars and dumbbells).

Core training is the latest buzzword amongst trainers, so you should have one or two exercises concentrating on the central sets of stabilising muscles in and around your trunk and back. For weight-loss programming these exercises should make up about 30% of your routine, and once you've achieved your fat-loss targets this may be an area your trainer needs to devote more time to.

You'll only need about 3–5 minutes of cardio warm-up before your weights routine as the prime purpose of this is to charge your blood and liver up with oxygen. However, the first set of every exercise should be performed with lighter weights than the next sets, and with a full range of movement to warm the muscles up through the movement you're about to do. So the first set of each exercise becomes a movement-specific warm-up.

Generally speaking the bigger movements for the larger muscle groups are done first in the routine while your energy and concentration levels are high, with the smaller muscle groups towards the end. These are exercises that are easier to perform, utilise lighter weights and don't require as much fuel to complete.

Most of your main weights exercises should be performed using a '10-rep max' formula. In layman's terms it's about lifting as much weight as you possibly can with correct form and safety for a maximum of 10 repetitions.

At all times you must maintain correct lifting timing and technique – no compromise. If you get sloppy or lift beyond your ability you will almost certainly injure yourself, and at the very least will not get as much out of the session. A good trainer will conduct a session with you on training safety and technique as part of your initial programme instruction. They should explain to you how to recognise good form in your own exercises, as well as explaining what to do to get out of an exercise quickly if you suddenly tire, injure yourself or lose your ability to control the weights.

In a nutshell
Phase 1
Weights: 3 x per week
Total body workout
@ 40 minutes, plus
20 minutes cardio
Cardio: 2 x per week
@ 40 minutes, building
up to 60 minutes

Phase 2
Weights: 2 x per
week @ 40 minutes,
plus 20 minutes cardio
Cardio: 3–4 x per
week at 60 minutes

Tim's training tips

- Get your muscles tuned up by lifting weights
- Allow one full day in between weights workouts
- Work on the bigger movements for your larger muscle groups first
- Work your smaller muscle groups towards the end of the routine
- Eat a small meal about one hour before training
- Try some classes for variety and fun
- Throw in some boxing training
- Do some cardio/aerobic training most days of the week to burn fat
- First thing in the morning is best for cardio work – on an empty stomach
- Sip on water – at a rate of about one litre per hour – when exercising
- Don't spend more than an hour in the gym at a time

Combination sessions

These are sessions that combine both weights and cardio training in the one workout. Examples are circuit training, TBC (total body conditioning) classes, BodyCombat®, and Bodypump® classes. They're an exciting way to exercise as a group or individually with your trainer, and very motivating. They generally involve a combination of strength, speed, agility, high-intensity fitness and aerobic fat-burning work, so kill a great many birds with the one stone. Additionally, your trainer may throw in some boxing training with you to keep the mix alive, challenging and interesting.

✓ **Don't get despondent by always focusing on the big goal. Go for smaller targets and the big one arrives more quickly**

✓ **A pedometer is an excellent fitness tool as it is your daily reminder of how active you actually are. It has been shown that taking 10,000 steps a day leads to more awareness of energy expenditure than a 30-minute walk. At less than £10 for a good basic model, they're a great investment in your overall plan**

✓ **Don't forget that short bouts of exercise (a brisk walk, for example) after a meal help reduce the fat in the bloodstream**

✓ **Your body is the only vehicle you have to carry you through your life. It needs preventative and knowledgeable servicing, just like a car**

✓ **You should have eaten a meal, containing protein and carbohydrate, about 60–90 minutes before a strength-training workout at the gym – a baked potato, tuna and salad, making sure to go for fat-free mayonnaise is one option. Or cajun turkey or chicken breast with brown rice, broccoli and two coloured vegetables of choice. You can also have a banana or a fruit snack or low-fat protein bar/shake 30 minutes before if you're feeling peckish. These pre-workout meals and snacks will allow you to have increased muscle strength, increased energy, burn more calories and fat and improve concentration**

✓ Exercise will never compensate for a diet that's too high in calories

✓ If you get embarrassed about your weight, do something about it

✓ Be proud that you have started to change destructive habits. It's all about you being in control of the way you look and feel and how you manage your environment

Strength (resistance) training addresses two core problems: the rate at which your body uses energy and the shape of your body. Instead of just going from being a big apple-shape to a small apple-shape (as you tend to do when dieting alone), with strength training you can sculpt a more flattering look to your body shape.

mythbuster

The Myth: *'Strength training makes you bigger and bulky.*

The Truth: Muscle takes up less room than fat within the body. Think of fat as a 5lb bag of potatoes and muscle as 5lbs of rice. The weight is the same but there is a big size difference.

In terms of body weight, the average adult changes 10lb per decade but their actual composition changes by approximately 20lb per decade. That's 15lbs MORE fat and 5lbs LESS muscle.

If you're already quite fit, go running outside

Drink 1.5–2.0 litres of water per day – it's good for your skin

hydration

Your body is 50–75% water. Without food, you could survive for six weeks. But without water you would die within a few days. Even mild dehydration can make you feel weak, dizzy and lacking in energy. Don't wait until you feel thirsty before you have a drink of water – thirst is a signal that your body is already on the way to dehydration, so it's important to drink more than your thirst demands and to keep on drinking throughout the day.

Over time, chronic dehydration can contribute to:

- Dry skin
- Constipation
- Kidney stones

You should drink 1.5–2.0 litres of water per day – that's about 8–10 good-sized glasses. You can get some of this from your food, particularly fresh, juicy foods like fruits and vegetables, but you'll need at least 1.8 litres from fluids, preferably pure water.

You can also count herb or fruit teas and diluted fruit juice towards your fluid intake. Tea and coffee also count. Because caffeine is a diuretic (it makes you pee, so you lose water) people used to think caffeine-containing drinks didn't count towards your fluid quota, but it's now believed that the water content of the drink more than offsets this. Just make sure your tea and coffee intake is moderate.

Fizzy drinks and squashes aren't recommended because of the sugars and artificial chemicals they contain. And alcohol certainly doesn't count when you're trying to reach your fluid target.

- Start with a glass of water first thing in the morning
- Buy a 2-litre bottle of mineral water, and keep refilling your glass, or using it to make hot drinks, throughout the day. You need to get through the whole bottle by bedtime. If you don't want to keep buying water, refill the bottle from the tap the next day
- Carry a small bottle of water with you when you're out and about
- If you're not used to drinking so much fluid, work up towards your target gradually to allow your body to adjust

getting a good night's sleep

While having the odd late night is unlikely to do more than make you feel a little cranky the next morning, regularly burning the candle at both ends or suffering from long-term insomnia will inevitably affect your quality of life. Sleep is the time when the pituitary gland in the brain pumps out growth hormone so that your body can synthesise new proteins for growth and repair.

Lack of sleep can:
- Suppress your immune system
- Lead to accidents
- Cause memory lapses
- Lead to an inability to concentrate

It is reported that Margaret Thatcher and Winston Churchill got by on just four hours sleep a night, but most of us need much longer if we are to be able to function efficiently.

But how much sleep do you really need? Although there are no hard and fast rules, it's generally accepted that most adults need about eight hours of shut-eye each night. The elderly tend to require less sleep and children considerably more.

Sleep stoppers
- *Alcohol. Although it may help you to get to sleep, it can disturb you later in the night*
- *A bedtime cigarette or a caffeine drink. You may think your last cigarette of the day relaxes you but in fact nicotine is a stimulant. Caffeine is also a stimulant so it's best avoided at night. If you are very sensitive to its effects you might be wise to give it a miss after lunchtime, or stick to decaff*
- *Eating a heavy meal less than three hours before bedtime*
- *Watching TV or having emotional discussions just before bedtime*

Tips for a restful night

- Make sure that your bedroom is relaxing, tidy and tranquil. Vivid colours and a collection of clutter are not conducive to relaxation and sleep

- If you experience traffic noise or light from street lamps invest in some ear plugs and heavy curtains or blinds for the windows

- A light snack at bedtime can help you sleep. Milk contains an amino acid (protein building block) called tryptophan which promotes sleep, and low-sugar biscuits or oatcakes help stabilise blood sugar levels

- Invest in a three-setting bedside lamp so that if you do wake in the night and need a bit of light, you can put it on a low level. A bright light can jolt you wide awake, making it more difficult to get back to sleep

- Try a few drops of lavender essential oil on your pillow

- Play some calming music or a relaxation tape

- Keep your bedroom temperature at a comfortable level

- Sleep with a window open if you can

- If you suffer from insomnia for more than a few days, see your doctor

CHAPTER 10

LIVE LONGER, LIVE BETTER

making the most of your longer life

UK Government figures reveal that girls born in 2004 can expect to live an average 81 years and boys an average 77. That's quite a contrast with life expectancy at the beginning of the twentieth century – just 45 years for men and 49 years for women.

That's the good news. Now for the bad. As well as living longer, we're living sicker. Statisticians can calculate the average number of years you can expect to live in poor health. In 1981, men could expect an average of 6.5 sick years, and women 10.1 sick years. But in 2001, men could look forward to 8.7 sick years, and women 11.6. So, although advances in medicine and drugs can keep you alive for longer, unless you take some action to lead a healthier lifestyle – to try to avoid the diseases that can strike as you get older – you may not be in a fit state to enjoy your extra time.

Get your brain in gear

Now that you've become more active and are providing your body with the right food and nutrients, it's time for some 'neuro-bics'. Get working on your brain's workout programme to preserve and enhance your mental skills. Improve your memory if you want a mind-active and fulfilled future.

You need to treat your brain like a muscle – and muscles need exercise. You can't turn back the tide and stop ageing altogether, but you can stop yourself feeling old and ageing prematurely.

Research has shown that people who keep their little grey cells active and maintain their interest in people and the world around them not only live longer but suffer less from depression and get more out of life.

Scientists have looked into why some healthy people retain their mental capabilities well into their seventies and eighties while others do not, and they discovered three key factors.

The high performers:

■ Had kept themselves more physically active
■ Were more mentally active – they read, did puzzles and were involved in hobbies and pastimes
■ Met challenges and change with confidence rather than being ground down by them

When researchers took 23 healthy people in their twenties and taught them to juggle, they found that after three months MRI scans showed an enlargement of the grey matter in their brains – the part responsible for higher mental functions. The scientists concluded that the existing cells in the brain had grown denser, more numerous connections had been established, or the number of brain cells had increased. But, whatever the reason, when the new jugglers stopped juggling their brains 'shrunk' again. This is just one study, but it does suggest that mental exercise has a positive and real effect on the brain.

The key to increasing your brain power is to take mental exercise as well as physical exercise. The more you're able to stimulate the brain by presenting it with exciting and new challenges the greater the benefits in later life. The brain is your body's master computer and you need to keep it working at top speed.

Things to do – NOW!

1 Take the 'I will' challenge. Set yourself challenges, whatever your age. 'I will learn to drive', 'I will learn to dance the salsa', 'I will conquer the mysteries of the computer', 'I will learn French.' When you reach your goals, use your new skills or they'll wane.

2 Take up crosswords, Sudoku, quizzes and wordsearches. Buy a puzzle book at the beginning of the month and try to finish it by the end of the month.

3 Enter competitions in magazines and newspapers.

4 Find some friends to play board games, Scrabble or card games with.

5 Make tracks. Travel broadens the mind, so hit the road. You don't have to head for the other side of the world, the other side of town is good enough. Visiting new places, experiencing new ways of living, discovering new foods, meeting new people all help to increase your brain power, your confidence and your feeling of well-being.

6 Check out your local learning centres and enrol in a class.

7 Keep the connections. You're designed to be a social animal not a lone cave dweller. It's tempting to switch on the television and slump alone in front of the box, but it's not a recipe for longevity. Get out, join a club, take up a hobby. Invest time in relationships with family and friends. Loners are more likely to smoke more cigarettes, eat less healthily and exercise less – another good reason to work on your social life.

8 Life's a laugh. When you reach adulthood it's easy to forget how to laugh, even though it does you the power of good. A really good laugh boosts the circulation and releases the endorphins – the natural painkillers – in your body. Research has shown that people with small circles of friends laugh less than those with a larger group.

9 Start looking on the bright side. Pessimism can be bad for your health. It's easy to see that having a mental attitude that assumes that the worst is bound to happen isn't conducive to happiness. Cultivating a positive mental attitude may not be easy but it will benefit your health. Don't sweat the small stuff – or the things that haven't happened and may never happen. Concentrate on the good things in your life.

10 Keep your eyes open for local lectures. Your local history society, natural history or geographical society is a good place to start. Look for details in your library or local newspaper.

11 Take up gardening. Being close to nature and away from the pressures of everyday life can lower your stress levels, and the pleasure of making things grow is hard to beat. If you put a bit of effort into it gardening can also give you a great physical workout.

12 Take yourself off to the library and scan the shelves for a good book. Get into the habit of trying to read at least one or two a month. If there's a book group there, think about joining it. It's a good place to meet people and to get talking.

13 Turn on the music. Music will help you relax. It can also reduce blood pressure, relieve tense muscles and help insomnia. Music therapy has been used to help treat depression and disturbed children.

14 Find a friend, set an agenda, settle down on the sofa and try to have at least one good discussion every week.

15 Stay cool. Most of us are able to withstand short periods of stress, but prolonged stress is harmful to the brain as well as the body. Practise your stress-busting techniques. See pp. 63–5 for tips.

use it or lose it

Try our brain maintenance quiz.

1 When did you last take up a new hobby?
[2] In the last year
[1] In the last 2 years
[0] I really can't remember

2 Do you attend any study classes?
[1] Yes
[0] No

3 Do you take part in any voluntary work?
[1] Yes
[0] No

4 Do you belong to any social or cultural organisations?
[1] Yes
[0] No

5 How many books do you read in a month?
[2] 3 or more a month
[1] 1–2
[0] None

6 Do you read newspapers, or watch or listen to news, current affairs and documentary programmes?
[2] Every day
[1] Occasionally
[0] Never

7 Would you describe yourself as a pessimist or an optimist?
[2] Optimist
[0] Pessimist

8 How often do you do a crossword puzzle, Sudoku puzzle or quiz?
[2] Every day
[1] Every week
[0] Less than once a week

9 When you are on holiday do you take the opportunity to explore?
[2] Always, it's what holidays are about
[1] I sometimes explore
[0] I stay on the beach and in the bars

10 How often do you visit places of interest like museums, castles and historic houses?
[2] At least once a month
[1] Only on holiday
[0] Never

Now add up your score.

12–17: Keep it up. Your brain is getting just the kind of workout it needs.

6–11: You are making a good effort, but try to find a few more activities to give your brain a boost.

Less than 6: Beware. You don't want to become mentally flabby! It's time to give your grey matter a workout.

Dr Una's top 10 anti-ageing tips

1 If you smoke, stop
2 Maintain a healthy weight
3 Get the exercise habit
4 Keep your brain active
5 Drink plenty of water
6 Eat oily fish at least twice a week (but no more than twice weekly if you're pregnant or planning a baby)
7 Maintain a normal blood pressure and low cholesterol
8 Snack on fruit
9 Switch from refined foods to wholemeal
10 Limit red meat to twice weekly (maximum)

In the past, people who lived to a hundred got there mainly through good genes and good luck. But you now have the advantage of knowing more about disease and the ageing process than ever before. And this gives you the power to make the kinds of life changes that will allow you to squeeze every last enjoyable day out of your life. It takes effort on your part, but it needn't be a chore, especially as you will very quickly start to feel the benefits.

Live longer,
Live healthier,
Live happier!

check it out

A number of health checks are available on the NHS and relatively few people take advantage of them. It's well worth getting them done if you are eligible. Spotting something nasty early could add years to your life.

Blood pressure

- Available for all men and women
- Every three years to the age of 50, then yearly

Why test? High blood pressure can increase the risk of stroke and heart disease. As there are often no symptoms, high blood pressure can be a silent killer.

Cholesterol

- Available for all men and women
- From age 40, every three years. Available earlier if heart disease runs in the family

Why test? High levels of LDL cholesterol can increase the risk of heart disease. It is estimated that 66% of adults in the UK have raised cholesterol levels.

Cervical smear

- All sexually active women aged 25–50 every three years. From 50–65 every five years
- Women over 65 only need to have a smear test if they have had an abnormal test, or have not had a test in the previous five years

Why test? To check for abnormal cells, which if left untreated could lead to cervical cancer.

Mammogram

- All women over 50 years, every three years
- Younger women can be screened if there is a history of breast cancer in the family

Why test? To detect changes in the breast which could indicate breast cancer.

Faecal occult blood test

- Men and women with a change in bowel habit or a family history of bowel cancer

Why test? To check for blood in the faeces that can't be spotted by eye – an indicator of bowel cancer. Early diagnosis increases the chance of a cure.

Fasting blood glucose

- If over 40 and overweight, especially if you have diabetes in the family

Why test? To check for diabetes, enabling treatment to start as soon as possible.

Chest X-ray and/or spirometry

- Heavy smoker, over 50, especially if you've never had these tests before

Why test? To check for lung cancer and COPD. See p. 80 for more information on lung problems.

Contact your GP to enquire about any of these tests. They may be carried out at the surgery or at a specialist screening clinic.

cosmetic surgery

Sooner or later, gravity comes calling on all of us. Skin starts to wrinkle, bits that were once pert and firm begin to sag. Everything makes a slow, inexorable journey south. There's an inevitability about sagging. It's part and parcel of growing older. So while you can do a lot to get your body and brain in shape you may find you want to 'nip and tuck' some remaining wobbly bits – particularly if you've lost a lot of weight.

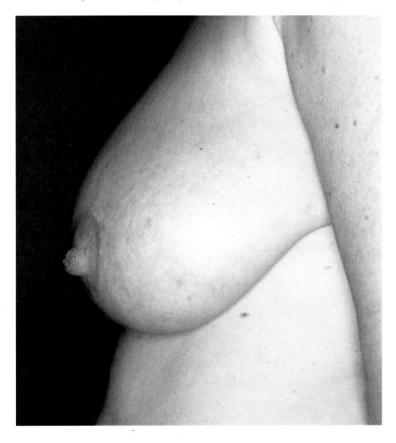

More and more people are going under the knife in an attempt to turn back the clock. It's your choice. Feeling better about your looks can give you the motivation to 'clean up' other areas of your life. Feeling happier and more being optimistic are good for you. Just be sure you're going under the knife for the right reasons.

Ask yourself these questions:

- Are you doing it for yourself (not for your partner, or to impress your friends or colleagues)?
- Are the changes you're after realistic?
- Will you be able to cope with the recuperation period and aftercare?
- Can you really afford the money, or will the expense put you under a lot of stress?

If you do decide to go ahead it's vital to arm yourself with all the information you can before you take the plunge. Cosmetic procedures can involve serious surgery – which can sometimes go wrong.

You need to know the answers to questions like:

- Who will carry out the treatment and what are their qualifications?
- Do they have professional indemnity insurance?
- How long does the treatment take?
- Is the treatment painful and if so what form of anaesthesia is used?
- What are the risks involved?
- What are the complications and success rate of the procedure in this clinic?
- Are there any other treatments available for me to achieve the results I want?
- What type of care will I need after treatment?
- How long do the results last?

The Department of Health has produced a lot of very useful and comprehensive information for anyone contemplating cosmetic surgery, including how to gather information and what questions to ask.

For more information visit **http://www.dh.gov.uk/PolicyAndGuidance/ HealthAndSocialCareTopics/CosmeticSurgery/fs/en**

APPENDIX 1

where to get help

General health information
NHS Direct: 0845 4647 and www.nhsdirect.nhs.uk/
For Scotland: *NHS 24:* 08454 24 24 24 and www.nhs24.com

Alcohol
Alcohol Concern: www.alcoholconcern.org.uk
Alcoholics Anonymous (24 hrs): 0845 769 7555
   and www.alcoholics-anonymous.org.uk
Drinkline: freephone 0800 917 8282

Blood pressure
British Hypertension Society: www.bhsoc.org

Cancer (general)
Cancer Help UK: 0207 061 8355 and www.cancerhelp.org.uk
Marie Curie Cancer Care: www.mariecurie.org.uk
Macmillan Cancer Relief: www.macmillan.org.uk

Cancers (specific)
Breast Cancer Care: 0808 800 6000 and www.breastcancercare.org.uk
Breakthrough Breast Cancer: www.breakthrough.org.uk
Roy Castle Lung Cancer Foundation: http://www.roycastle.org
The Prostate Cancer Charity: 0845 300 8383 and www.prostate-cancer.org.uk
British Skin Foundation (for information on skin cancer):
   www.britishskinfoundation.org.uk

Diabetes
Diabetes UK Careline: 0845 120 2960 and www.diabetes.org.uk

Drugs
National Drugs Helpline (24hrs): 0800 77 66 00
Drugscope: www.drugscope.org.uk

Heart problems

British Heart Foundation: 08450 70 80 70 and www.bhf.org.uk

Liver problems

British Liver Trust: 0870 770 8028 and www.britishlivertrust.org.uk
UK Transplant: www.uktransplant.org.uk

Lung problems

Lung UK: 08458 50 50 20 and www.lunguk.org.uk
Asthma UK: 08457 01 02 03 and www.asthma.org.uk

Organic food

The Soil Association: www.soilassociation.org.uk

Osteoporosis

National Osteoporosis Society: 01761 471771 and www.nos.org.uk

Slow food

The Slow Food Movement: www.slowfood.com

Smoking

Action on Smoking and Health (ASH): www.ash.org.uk
NHS Smoking Helpline: 0800 169 0 169
*Pregnancy Quitline (for pregnant woman seeking
    help to stop smoking):* 0800 169 9169

Stroke

The Stroke Association: 0845 3033 100 and www.stroke.org.uk

APPENDIX 2

the lunch recipes

week 1

DAY 1

Salmon and cucumber wholemeal sandwich
1 portion of fruit or raw vegetable sticks

2 slices wholemeal bread
1 small tin salmon, drained, skin removed
3-inch piece cucumber, skinned, seeds removed, finely chopped
Handful of salad leaves
2 tsp low-fat salad cream
Splash of vinegar (optional)
Freshly ground black pepper

Spread one teaspoon of the salad cream over the 2 slices of bread.
In a small bowl combine the salmon, cucumber, the remaining salad
cream, the splash of vinegar if used, and freshly ground black pepper.
Arrange the salad leaves over one slice of bread. Spread the salmon
filling over the second piece of bread. Cut the sandwich into two and
wrap in clingfilm. Chill until needed.

DAY 2

Wholemeal turkey and cranberry sandwich
1 portion of fruit or raw vegetable sticks

2 slices wholemeal bread
2 slices roast turkey
1 tsp cranberry sauce
1 tomato, sliced
Freshly ground black pepper
Handful of salad leaves
A little low-fat spread

Lightly spread the bread with low-fat spread, then top with the salad leaves and sliced tomato. Add the turkey slices and cranberry sauce. Season with black pepper. Wrap and chill until needed.

DAY 3

Cottage cheese with pineapple, salad and crispbreads
1 portion of fruit or raw vegetable sticks

100g cottage cheese with pineapple
5 rye crispbreads
Handful of salad leaves
Large tomato, cut into wedges
Cucumber slices
Celery
Splash of fat-free vinaigrette

Place the salad vegetables in a lidded container, with the cottage cheese on top. Sprinkle on a little dressing (or take with you to add later).

DAY 4

Egg and potato salad served with wholemeal roll
1 portion of fruit or fresh vegetable sticks

1 hard-boiled egg, cooled, cut into wedges
1 grated carrot
4 small, cooked new potatoes, sliced
1 tbsp low-fat coleslaw
2-inch piece cucumber, sliced
1 tomato, cut into wedges
Large handful of shredded lettuce or salad leaves

Place the salad leaves in the bottom of a lidded container. Arrange the other salad vegetables over. Then add the sliced potato, egg pieces and the coleslaw. Lightly spread the wholemeal roll with a low-fat spread.

DAY 5

Tuna pasta salad
1 portion of fruit or raw vegetable sticks

40g cooked pasta
2 tbsp chopped cooked beetroot
50g flaked tinned tuna
½ green pepper, diced
2 spring onions, finely chopped
1 tomato, deseeded and chopped
2 tbsp sweetcorn
2 tbsp yoghurt or fat-free vinaigrette
Ground black pepper

Combine the ingredients and place in a lidded container. Chill until needed.

DAY 6

Soft cheese, banana and runny honey on granary roll
1 portion of fruit or raw vegetable sticks

1 granary roll
½ large banana, sliced
20g low-fat soft cheese
1 tsp runny honey

Cut the granary roll in half and spread both sides of the granary roll with the soft cheese. Arrange the slices of banana over one half of the roll then drizzle over the honey.

DAY 7

Roasted mediterranean vegetables, feta cheese and
    salad leaves in a wrap
1 portion of fruit or raw vegetable sticks

3 tbsp roasted Mediterranean vegetables
1 tomato, halved and sliced
6 cucumber slices, cut into quarters
Handful of shredded lettuce or salad leaves

2 tbsp low-fat natural yoghurt
Freshly ground black pepper
15g feta cheese, crumbled

Arrange the lettuce or salad leaves over the wrap. Add the cucumber and tomato. Combine the Mediterranean vegetables, the yoghurt and black pepper and spoon over the salad vegetables. Sprinkle over the crumbled feta cheese and roll up the wrap.

week 2

DAY 1

Soft cheese and carrot granary sandwich
1 portion of fruit or raw vegetable sticks

2 slices granary or wholemeal bread
20g low-fat soft cheese
½ grated carrot
2 finely chopped dried apricots
4 chopped walnuts

Spread both slices of bread with the low-fat soft cheese. Top with the carrot and sprinkle over the apricots and chopped walnuts.

DAY 2

Tuna and salad pitta
1 portion of fruit or raw vegetable sticks

1 wholemeal pitta
50g flaked tinned tuna
1 tbsp low-fat natural yoghurt
Freshly ground black pepper
Squeeze of lemon (optional)
2 spring onions, finely chopped
1 tomato, halved and sliced
6 slices of cucumber cut into quarters
½ red pepper, deseeded and sliced

Handful of lettuce or salad leaves

Cut the pitta in half and open into pockets. Arrange the lettuce or salad leaves in the pockets. In a small bowl combine the flaked tuna, yoghurt, spring onions, red pepper, tomato and cucumber. Add the yoghurt, black pepper and lemon juice, if used. Spoon into the pockets. Wrap each half in clingfilm.

DAY 3

Tuna (or salmon), sweetcorn and red or yellow pepper wholemeal sandwich
1 portion of fruit or raw vegetable sticks

2 slices wholemeal bread
2 tbsp sweetcorn
½ red or yellow pepper, deseeded and finely chopped
50g flaked tinned tuna (or salmon if preferred)
2 tbsp low-fat mayonnaise
Freshly ground black pepper
Handful of salad leaves or lettuce

Spread each slice of bread with half of the mayonnaise. Arrange the salad leaves on one slice of the bread. Combine the tuna, chopped pepper and sweetcorn in a bowl, and spoon on to the sandwich. Season with black pepper. Chill until needed.

DAY 4

Ham and mustard sandwich on wholemeal submarine roll
1 portion of fruit or raw vegetable sticks

1 wholemeal submarine roll
2 slices cooked ham
1 tomato, sliced
Handful of shredded lettuce or salad leaves
English or Dijon mustard to taste

Lightly spread the roll with mustard to taste. Place the ham slices over the mustard. Add the lettuce or salad leaves and tomato slices. Wrap and chill until needed.

DAY 5

Roast chicken with salad, coleslaw and granary roll
1 portion of fruit or raw vegetable sticks

40g roast chicken, cut into bite-sized pieces
1 grated carrot
2 tbsp low-fat coleslaw
2-inch piece cucumber, sliced
1 tomato, cut into wedges
Large handful of shredded lettuce or salad leaves

Place the lettuce or salad leaves in the bottom of a lidded container.
Arrange the other salad vegetables over. Add the roast chicken and
the coleslaw. Lightly spread the roll with a low-fat spread.

DAY 6

Cottage cheese with peach and salad, with 5 wholemeal crispbreads
1 portion of fruit or raw vegetable sticks

100g cottage cheese
1 tinned peach half, drained (tinned in juice not syrup)
1 small grated carrot
2-inch piece cucumber, sliced
1 tomato, cut into wedges
1 stick of celery, cut into small pieces
Large handful of shredded lettuce or salad leaves
5 rye crispbreads

Place the lettuce or salad leaves in the bottom of a lidded container.
Arrange the other salad vegetables over. Add the cottage cheese and
the peach cut into small pieces.

DAY 7

Brown rice and vegetable salad with chicken, tuna or ham
1 portion of fruit or raw vegetable sticks

40g cooked brown rice
½ pepper, finely diced
½ carrot, finely diced

1 tomato, deseeded and finely sliced
2-inch piece cucumber, skinned, seeds removed and finely diced
2 spring onions, finely chopped
Handful of shredded lettuce or salad leaves
2 small slices chicken, ham or 30g flaked tinned tuna
A little oil-free dressing
Freshly ground black pepper

Combine all of the ingredients gently in a bowl. Transfer to a lidded container and chill until needed.

week 3

DAY 1

Curried chicken wrap
1 portion of fruit or raw vegetable sticks

2 wholemeal wraps (such as fajita or chapattis)
2 tbsp cold cooked chicken, chopped
1 tsp curry paste
2 tsp low-fat natural yoghurt
1 tomato, halved and thinly sliced
8 slices cucumber
Handful of shredded lettuce or baby salad leaves

Combine the chopped chicken, yoghurt and curry paste in a small bowl. Lay the lettuce or salad leaves on the wrap and add the other ingredients. Roll the wrap, cut in half and wrap each half in clingfilm. Chill until needed. (Make sure you use a curry paste that does not have to be cooked. If you can't find one, use ½ tsp curry powder.)

DAY 2

Bagel with low-fat cream cheese and salmon and salad
1 portion of fruit or raw vegetable sticks

1 wholemeal or plain bagel
20g smoked salmon

40g low-fat cream cheese
1 small grated carrot
2-inch piece cucumber, sliced
1 tomato, cut into wedges
1 stick celery, cut into small pieces
Large handful of shredded lettuce or salad leaves
A little fat-free vinaigrette (optional)

Split the bagel in half and spread with the cream cheese. Cut the salmon into small pieces and arrange over the cheese. Sandwich the bagel together. Place the lettuce or salad leaves in the bottom of a lidded container. Arrange the other salad vegetables over. Add a little dressing, if needed.

DAY 3

Small tin mackerel or sardines in tomato sauce, salad and a granary roll
1 portion of fruit or raw vegetable sticks

2 large handfuls of mixed salad leaves
2 small boiled new potatoes, sliced
2 spring onions, finely sliced
1 stick celery, chopped
1 small tin mackerel or sardines in tomato sauce
1 granary roll
A little low-fat spread

Place the salad leaves in the bottom of a lidded container. Arrange the other vegetables over. Spoon the mackerel or sardines on to the salad. Chill until needed. Spread the granary roll with a little low-fat spread, if required.

DAY 4

Nutty cheese pitta
1 portion of fruit or raw vegetable sticks

1 wholemeal pitta
A handful of salad leaves
20g grated mature Cheddar

1 tbsp chopped walnuts
½ chopped apple
1 tomato, deseeded and chopped
1 tsp low-fat mayonnaise

Cut the pitta in half and open into pockets. Line with the salad leaves. Combine the other ingredients in a small bowl and spoon into the pockets. Wrap in clingfilm and chill until needed

DAY 5

Light egg mayo on wholemeal submarine roll
1 portion of fruit or raw vegetable sticks

1 egg, hard-boiled and chopped
1 tsp low-fat mayonnaise
1 finely chopped spring onion
1 tomato, deseeded and chopped
Small handful lettuce, finely shredded
Freshly ground black pepper

Combine the ingredients, except the lettuce, in a small bowl. Cut the roll in half lengthways and spread the filling on both sides. Add the shredded lettuce and sandwich the roll together. Wrap in clingfilm and chill until needed.

DAY 6

Tuna, chopped tomato, and watercress on wholemeal bread
1 portion of fruit or raw vegetable sticks

50g flaked tinned tuna
1 large tomato, deseeded and thinly sliced
Handful of watercress, washed
1 tsp low-fat mayonnaise
2 slices wholemeal bread
Freshly ground black pepper

Spread both slices of the bread with the low-fat mayonnaise. Arrange the tomato slices over one slice of bread, then add the tuna and the watercress. Season with ground black pepper.

DAY 7

Roast beef and horseradish sandwich, with tomato and salad leaves on wholemeal submarine roll
1 portion of fruit or raw vegetable sticks

1 wholemeal submarine roll
1 large tomato, sliced
2 small slices of roast beef
1 tsp horseradish sauce
Handful of shredded lettuce or salad leaves
Freshly ground black pepper

Split the roll in half and spread both sides with the horseradish sauce. Top with the slices of roast beef, tomato and lettuce or salad leaves. Season with ground black pepper.

week 4

DAY 1

Tofu sausage and salad bowl
1 portion of fruit or raw vegetable sticks

1 tofu (or Quorn®) sausage, grilled, cooled and sliced
1 small carrot, grated
2-inch piece cucumber, sliced
1 tomato, cut into wedges
2 small new cooked boiled potatoes
½ red or green pepper, deseeded and sliced
Large handful of shredded lettuce or salad leaves
1 tsp low-fat salad dressing

Arrange the salad leaves in the base of a lidded container. Arrange the other salad vegetables and potato over. Arrange the sausage slices on the top of the salad. Spoon on the salad dressing. Chill until needed.

DAY 2

Shredded chicken and salad bowl
1 portion of fruit or raw vegetable sticks

50g cooked chicken, shredded
1 tsp sandwich pickle
1 small grated carrot
2-inch piece cucumber, sliced
1 tomato, cut into wedges
1 stick celery, cut into small pieces
½ red or green pepper, deseeded and sliced
Large handful of shredded lettuce or salad leaves

Arrange the shredded lettuce or salad leaves in a lidded container.
Then add the remaining salad vegetables. Arrange the chicken on
the top and add the pickle. Chill until needed.

DAY 3

Spicy stir-fried chicken and salad wrap
1 portion of fruit or raw vegetable sticks

1 wholemeal fajita wrap
2 tbsp spicy stir-fried chicken
½ pepper, cut into strips
1 tomato, sliced
Handful of lettuce, shredded
2 tbsp low-fat natural yoghurt
Freshly ground black pepper

Arrange the lettuce over the wrap. Add the pepper strips and the
tomato. Combine the spicy chicken, the yoghurt and the black
pepper and spoon over the salad filling. Roll the wrap and cut into
two. Wrap in clingfilm and chill until ready to serve.

DAY 4

Garlic cheese and salad wholemeal sandwich
1 portion of fruit or raw vegetable sticks

20g low-fat garlic cheese
1 tomato, sliced
6 slices of cucumber
Handful of shredded lettuce or salad leaves
2 slices wholemeal bread

Spread both slices of the bread with the garlic cheese. Arrange the tomato and cucumber slices over. Top with the lettuce or salad leaves.

DAY 5

Salmon and cucumber wholemeal sandwich
1 portion of fruit or raw vegetable sticks

2 slices wholemeal bread
1 small tin salmon, drained, skin removed
3-inch piece cucumber, skinned, seeds removed, finely chopped
Handful of salad leaves
2 tsp low-fat salad cream
Splash of vinegar (optional)
Freshly ground black pepper

Spread one teaspoon of the salad cream over the 2 slices of bread. In a small bowl combine the salmon, cucumber, the remaining salad cream, the splash of vinegar if used, and freshly ground black pepper. Arrange the salad leaves over one slice of bread. Spread the salmon filling over the second piece of bread. Cut the sandwich into two and wrap in clingfilm. Chill until needed.

DAY 6

Wholemeal turkey and cranberry sandwich
1 portion of fruit or raw vegetable sticks

See p. 193 for the recipe.

DAY 7

Soft cheese and grated carrot granary sandwich
1 portion of fruit or raw vegetable sticks

See p. 197 for the recipe.

APPENDIX 3

the dinner recipes

week 1

DAY 1
Jacket potato with curried bean filling

1 baking potato
½ small onion
Small tin baked beans (low sugar, low salt)
1 tomato, diced
1 tsp mild curry paste

1 Microwave the jacket potato until cooked.
2 Meanwhile make the filling. Fry the onion in a non-stick saucepan
until softened, add the diced tomato and the curry paste and cook for
a minute. Add the beans and heat through. Cut a cross in the top of
the potato and fill with the bean mixture.
3 Serve with a large mixed salad.

DAY 2
Pan-fried cod

1 small cod steak
1 tsp olive oil
Ground black pepper

1 Put a little oil on both sides of the cod steak. Place in a non-stick
pan and cook on both sides for 2–3 minutes until the fish is cooked.
2 Serve with three small boiled new potatoes and a mixture of
steamed fresh vegetables.

DAY 3
Stir-fried beef with broccoli

8 small broccoli florets
½ red pepper, deseeded and sliced
3 spring onions
80g sirloin steak, cut into thin strips
1 clove garlic, finely chopped
1 tbsp light soy sauce
1 tsp honey
1 tbsp water
1 tsp olive oil

1 Heat the oil in a wok or large frying pan. Add the vegetables and fry for 2 minutes stirring all the time. Add the garlic and the water and cook for a further minute.
2 Add the steak, soy sauce and honey and cook for 1–2 minutes until the beef is just cooked.
3 Serve on a bed of brown rice or noodles.

DAY 4
Spicy prawns and spaghetti

50g cooked frozen prawns, defrosted
40g spaghetti
½ red pepper, deseeded and finely chopped
2 spring onions, finely chopped
1 clove garlic, crushed
1 tbsp chopped fresh parsley
½ tsp dried chilli flakes to taste
Ground black pepper
1 small tin tomatoes

1 Cook the spaghetti according to the packet instructions.
2 Meanwhile lightly oil a non-stick pan and fry the spring onions, red pepper, garlic and chilli flakes for one minute. Add the tomatoes and cook for three minutes. Stir in the parsley and the prawns and cook until the prawns are heated through.

3 Drain the pasta and add to the sauce.

4 Serve immediately with a large mixed salad.

DAY 5

Hot and sweet chicken

1 small boneless chicken breast, skinned

1 tsp sweet pickle

½ tsp olive oil

½ tsp English mustard

½ tsp honey

½ tsp tomato puree (optional)

1 Preheat the oven to 180°C/gas mark 4.

2 Place the chicken breast on a piece of foil. Combine the other ingredients in a small bowl and spoon over the breast. Cover the chicken with the foil to make a loose parcel. Bake in the oven for 20–25 minutes, or until the chicken is thoroughly cooked.

3 Serve with three small boiled new potatoes, green beans and a grilled or baked tomato.

DAY 6

Salmon and sweetcorn salad

100g can salmon, skinned, drained and flaked

½ small can sweetcorn

1 shallot, finely chopped

50g tinned kidney beans, washed and drained

½ red pepper, deseeded and chopped

Large handful of shredded lettuce

1 tsp olive oil

1 tsp vinegar

1 Combine all of the ingredients in a bowl and toss lightly. Arrange on a plate and drizzle over the oil and vinegar.

2 Serve with a toasted crusty wholemeal roll.

DAY 7
Speedy cheesy pasta

40g penne pasta or similar
80g green beans, trimmed and halved
6 cherry tomatoes, halved
3 tbsp skimmed milk
20g low-fat garlic and herb cheese
½ tbsp chopped parsley (optional)

1 Cook the pasta according to the directions on the packet.
Drain and return to the saucepan.
2 Cook the green beans, drain and add to the pasta. Then add the
halved cherry tomatoes, the skimmed milk and the garlic and herb
cheese. Cook over a low heat until everything is warmed through
and the cheese has melted.
3 Serve with a large green salad with parsley sprinkled on top, if liked.

week 2

DAY 1
Mustard chicken

1 small chicken breast, skinned
1 tsp wholegrain mustard
½ tsp chopped rosemary
1 tsp lemon juice
1 clove garlic, crushed
½ tsp olive oil

1 Marinade the chicken in the other ingredients.
2 Grill or griddle the chicken until it is completely cooked through.
3 Serve with 3 small boiled new potatoes and a large mixed salad or
mixed fresh vegetables.

DAY 2
Simple vegetable and chickpea stew

1 stick celery, chopped
½ red pepper, deseeded and chopped
½ small onion, chopped
1 carrot, chopped
1 small can chopped tomatoes
1 sprig rosemary or mixed herbs
50g green beans, halved
450ml vegetable stock
½ can chickpeas, drained and well rinsed
1 tbsp chopped parsley
Freshly ground black pepper

1 Lightly oil a large saucepan. Fry all of the fresh vegetables, except
the green beans, for 2 minutes. Add the tinned tomatoes, rosemary or
mixed herbs and stock. Season with ground black pepper. Cover and
simmer gently for 30 minutes. Add the green beans and chickpeas and
cook for a further 10 minutes.
2 Serve with new potatoes (or pasta) and a green salad.

DAY 3
Grilled chicken breast with tomato and sweetcorn mash

1 small chicken breast, skin removed
1 small can sweetcorn, no sugar or salt added
6 cherry tomatoes, halved
100g mashed potato (no butter)
Cajun seasoning

1 Sprinkle a little Cajun seasoning on the chicken breast and grill
or griddle until the chicken is cooked. Add the cherry tomatoes to
the grill or griddle for the last 2 minutes of cooking time.
2 Drain the sweetcorn and stir into the mashed potato.
Keep warm until ready to serve.
3 Serve with green beans and broccoli or a large mixed salad.

DAY 4

Butter beans with mushrooms and cherry tomatoes

1 small can butter beans, rinsed and drained
1 small onion, chopped
1 clove garlic, crushed
50g mushrooms, wiped and sliced
6 cherry tomatoes
80g green beans
2 pinches of dried thyme
100ml stock or water
1 tbsp yoghurt (optional)
Freshly ground black pepper

1 Lightly oil a saucepan. Add the onion and garlic and cook gently until softened. Add the mushrooms, the tomatoes, the dried thyme and the stock or water and bring to the boil. Put a lid on the pan and turn the heat down to the lowest setting. Simmer for 15 minutes. (Check that the liquid has not evaporated during the cooking time and if necessary add a little more.)
2 Add the butter beans and cook gently for 5 minutes. Add the yoghurt to the sauce, if liked.
3 Serve with mashed or boiled new potatoes and fresh vegetables.

DAY 5

Crusty cod with cheese and tomato

150g cod (or haddock) fillet
1 tomato, sliced
1 clove garlic, crushed
Zest and juice of half a lemon
1 tbsp freshly chopped parsley
15g mature half-fat Cheddar, grated
½ slice wholemeal bread, crumbed
Ground black pepper
1 tsp olive oil

1 Preheat oven to 180°C/gas mark 4.
2 Place the breadcrumbs, parsley, lemon zest, oil and garlic in a bowl

and combine.

3 Lightly oil a shallow ovenproof dish and place the fish in the middle. Top with the tomato slices, then press the breadcrumb mixture on the top. Scatter the grated cheese over. Bake for 12–15 minutes until the fish is just cooked and the topping crisp.

4 Serve with boiled new potatoes and fresh vegetables.

DAY 6

Honey and mustard salmon

1 small skinless salmon fillet

1 tsp runny honey

1 tsp light soy sauce

1 tbsp lime or lemon juice

1 tsp wholegrain mustard

2 tbsp water

1 spring onion, finely shredded

1 Combine the honey, soy sauce, lime or lemon juice, wholegrain mustard and water in a small bowl.

2 Heat a non-stick frying pan and add the salmon (do not add any oil). Cook for 3–4 minutes and then turn the salmon over. Pour the honey mixture over and allow to bubble for 1–2 minutes.

3 Remove the salmon on to a serving plate and pour over the sauce. Pile the shredded spring onion on to the salmon.

4 Serve with new potatoes, green beans and broccoli.

DAY 7

Chickpea and vegetable chilli

1 small can chickpeas

1 small onion, chopped

1 small clove garlic, crushed

1 small can tomatoes

½ tsp sugar

100ml vegetable stock

¼ tsp chilli powder (or to taste)

1 carrot, chopped

6 cauliflower florets

½ red pepper, deseeded and chopped
6 broccoli florets
1 tbsp low-fat natural yoghurt (optional)

1 Lightly oil a saucepan and fry the onion for 5 or 6 minutes until golden. Add the garlic and spices and cook for a further minute. Add the stock and sugar. Add the chickpeas and vegetables and simmer until the vegetables are tender (about 10 minutes).
2 Just before serving stir in the yoghurt, if used.
3 Serve with pasta and a mixed salad.

week 3

DAY 1
Quick Balti fruity chicken curry

1 chicken breast, skin removed and cut into thin slices
1 onion, halved and finely sliced
1 clove garlic, finely chopped
50g green beans
6 cauliflower florets
4 cherry tomatoes, halved
1 slice pineapple, chopped
1 tbsp sultanas or raisins (optional)
1–2 tsp Balti curry paste (according to taste)
2 large handfuls of baby spinach leaves, washed
100ml water

1 Stir-fry the chicken, onion and garlic for 5 minutes. Add the Balti paste and cook for 2 minutes. Add half of the water and cook for a further 5 minutes. Add the green beans, cauliflower, cherry tomatoes and pineapple and the rest of the water and cook for 10 minutes. Add the spinach leaves and cook for 1–2 minutes until the spinach is wilted.
2 Serve with brown rice and a mixed salad.

DAY 2

Fresh tuna (or salmon) with lime and chilli

150g fresh tuna steak (or salmon)
½ small red chilli, seeds removed
Zest and juice of half a lime
1 clove garlic, finely chopped
1 tsp olive oil
Ground black pepper

1 Place all the ingredients on to a plate and marinade the tuna steak for 5 minutes, turning once. Season with ground black pepper.
2 Remove the tuna from the marinade. Lightly oil a non-stick griddle or frying pan and cook the steak for 2–3 minutes on each side depending on the thickness.
3 Serve with boiled new potatoes or brown rice, and steamed vegetables.

DAY 3

Spicy bean or lentil casserole

½ can mixed beans or lentils, drained and rinsed
1 small onion, chopped
1 small can chopped tomatoes
¼ tsp paprika or mild chilli powder
50g mushrooms, quartered
1 green pepper, deseeded and diced
100ml water or stock
1 tbsp natural low-fat yoghurt (optional)
1 tbsp chopped fresh coriander

1 Lightly oil a saucepan and fry the onion. Add the mushrooms, tomatoes and pepper and the water or stock. Add the paprika or chilli powder and the beans or lentils. Bring to the boil, lower the heat and simmer for 15 minutes. Turn into a dish, add the tablespoon of natural yoghurt and the fresh coriander.
2 Serve with a green salad or fresh vegetables.

DAY 4

Spicy lamb chop with couscous and mixed salad

1 100g lamb steak, fat removed
½ tsp Cajun spice
40g plain couscous

1 Rub the Cajun spice on both sides of the meat.
2 Grill or griddle the meat until cooked.
3 Make a portion of couscous according to the instructions on the packet, using low-salt vegetable stock.
4 Serve with a large mixed salad.

DAY 5

Quick Mediterranean chicken casserole

1 small chicken breast, skin removed, cut into four slices
1 small onion, chopped
1 clove garlic, crushed
1 tsp tomato puree
150ml chicken stock or water
1 small can chopped mushrooms
½ tsp sugar
50g green beans, topped and tailed and halved
Freshly ground black pepper
1 tsp Worcestershire sauce (optional)
8 stoned olives (optional)
1 tsp chopped parsley

1 Lightly oil a non-stick saucepan and fry the chicken pieces until coloured, and the onion and garlic until softened slightly. Add the tomato puree, sugar, ground black pepper, chopped tomatoes and water or stock to the pan. Put a lid on the saucepan and simmer gently for 20 minutes. Add the green beans and cook for a further 15 minutes.
2 Add the olives and Worcestershire sauce if used, and scatter the parsley on the top. Simmer for another 5 minutes.
3 Serve with boiled potatoes, pasta or a crusty wholemeal roll and fresh vegetables.

DAY 6
Mushroom omelette

2 medium eggs
1 tbsp water
8 button mushrooms, peeled and sliced
1 tsp chopped fresh parsley
Salt and pepper
1 tsp olive oil

1 Beat the eggs with the water in a bowl.
2 Gently stir-fry the mushrooms in a little water in a small frying pan. Remove from the pan.
3 Lightly wipe the pan with olive oil and heat gently. Add the egg mixture and cook until the bottom of the omelette is lightly browned and the top is beginning to set. Add the mushrooms and fold the omelette in half. Cook for a further minute.
4 Serve with 3 small boiled new potatoes and 2 grilled tomatoes and a small can of sweetcorn.

DAY 7
Speedy Oriental Quorn®

1 bag of Oriental stir-fry vegetables
100g Quorn® chunks
1 small onion, halved and finely sliced
1 tsp olive oil
1 tsp soy sauce
½ tsp Chinese 5-spice powder (optional)
Squeeze of lemon (optional)
2–4 tbsp water or stock
Freshly ground black pepper

1 Heat a teaspoon of olive oil in a wok or large frying pan and add the Quorn® chunks and onion. Cook for a couple of minutes. Add the stir-fry vegetables, the water or stock and spice powder and cook for 2–3 more minutes. Add the soy sauce and lemon juice, and stir.
2 Serve immediately with brown rice.

week 4

DAY 1

Spanish chicken

1 small chicken breast, skin removed
1 small green pepper, deseeded and sliced
1 small onion, sliced
1 clove garlic, crushed
Small tin tomatoes
½ tsp dried oregano or mixed herbs
1 tbsp fresh basil, chopped (optional)
100ml chicken stock
8 green or black olives, stoned
Freshly ground black pepper

1 Fry the chicken breast in a non-stick pan for about 2 minutes
each side to seal. Add the onion and pepper and cook for 5 minutes
until beginning to brown. Add the garlic, tinned tomatoes, dried herbs,
olives, black pepper and stock. Reduce heat, place a lid on the pan
and simmer gently for 30 minutes until the chicken is tender. (Check
once or twice to see that the liquid has not evaporated and add a little
water if necessary.)
2 Spoon on to a plate and sprinkle over the basil, if used.
3 Serve with a portion of penne pasta or spaghetti and a green salad.

DAY 2

Garlic and chilli prawn stir-fry

100g frozen prawns, defrosted
2 cloves garlic
1 small onion, finely chopped
½ tsp chilli flakes, to taste
1 large tomato, finely chopped
1 tbsp chopped parsley
4 tbsp water
Freshly ground black pepper

1 Lightly oil a non-stick pan and gently fry the onion and garlic for 2 minutes. Add the tomato and the water and continue to cook until the tomato has softened and formed a sauce.

2 Add the prawns and heat through – do not overcook or the prawns will be tough. Season with pepper and stir in the parsley.

3 Serve with wholemeal rice or a crusty roll and a large mixed salad.

DAY 3

Spicy veggie burgers

(Makes 4 burgers – eat one and freeze the remainder to use later)

1 medium onion, finely chopped
¼ tsp ready prepared 'lazy' chilli
2 sticks celery, very finely chopped
2 cloves garlic, crushed
2 slices wholemeal bread, grated
2 x 420g can kidney beans, washed and drained
2 eggs, beaten
Freshly ground black pepper

1 Spray a non-stick pan with a very small quantity of oil. Fry the celery and onion until softened. Tip into a mixing bowl.

2 Mash the kidney beans and add to the mixing bowl. Add the remaining ingredients. Form into four burgers.

3 To cook a burger place it in a lightly oiled non-stick pan and cook for 3 minutes on each side. Serve on half of a toasted wholemeal burger bap spread with chutney. Top with tomato slices and a chopped salad gherkin.

4 Serve with a large mixed salad.

DAY 4

Chicken with pepper salsa

1 small chicken breast, skinned
½ red pepper, finely chopped
½ green pepper, finely chopped
½ small red chilli, seeds removed, finely chopped
2 spring onions, finely chopped

2 tsp lemon juice

½ tsp mint sauce (optional)

1 Combine all the salsa ingredients in a small bowl.

2 Bake, grill or griddle the chicken until thoroughly cooked.

3 Put the chicken on a plate and spoon over the salsa.

4 Serve with a large mixed salad.

DAY 5

Quick spicy tofu sausage and beans

1 tofu (or Quorn®) sausage

1 small onion, chopped

1 small tin reduced-sugar, low-salt baked beans

1 small can chopped tomatoes

1–2 tsp Worcestershire sauce

1 clove garlic (optional)

1 Lightly spray a non-stick frying pan with a small amount of oil and cook the sausage. Set aside.

2 Add the onion and garlic and cook until lightly golden. Add the beans and the tomatoes and cook for 3 or 4 minutes. Stir in the Worcestershire sauce and return the sausage to the pan. Cook for 2 or 3 minutes to heat through.

3 Serve with mashed potatoes (no butter) or brown rice and plenty of fresh vegetables.

DAY 6

Grilled steak with horseradish mash

90g sirloin steak, fat removed

5 cherry tomatoes, halved

100g potato, boiled and mashed (no butter)

½ tsp horseradish sauce

Freshly ground black pepper

1 Lightly oil a griddle pan. Season the steak with pepper and cook it to rare, medium or well done, according to taste. Add the halved cherry tomatoes for the last two minutes of cooking time.

2 Beat the horseradish sauce into the mashed potato.

3 Serve with a large mixed salad or a selection of fresh vegetables.

DAY 7

Vegetable and lentil stew

½ can green lentils, rinsed and drained
1 small onion, chopped
1 small red pepper, deseeded and sliced
1 clove garlic
½ small courgette, sliced in rings
1 small can chopped tomatoes
¼ tsp crushed dried chilli, or more if liked
1 tsp oil
50ml water or stock
Freshly ground black pepper
1 tbsp natural yoghurt (optional)

1 Lightly oil a saucepan and gently fry the onion, dried chilli and garlic for 2 minutes. Add the tomatoes, pepper and courgette, lentils and stock and simmer for 10 minutes.

2 Season with pepper and simmer for a further 5 minutes. Stir in the yoghurt, if used.

3 Serve immediately with new potatoes or pasta and a green salad.